# LOW-CARB
# VEGETARIAN

# LOW-CARB VEGETARIAN

celia brooks brown

photography by tara fisher
nutritional analysis by fiona hunter

whitecap

# contents

# introduction

**"Have you heard about this great new diet? No third helpings."** Stanley Kubrick

It was Stanley Kubrick's wife Christiane who first got me started on this book. I cook for her, her family and friends nearly every week, so when several of them decided to try a low-carb diet, it was time for me to get my low-carb thinking cap on. This is the result of many months experimenting, learning, feasting, and losing weight!

This is not a diet book, it's a cookbook. That said, it's a cookbook mainly for those who have embraced the low-carb lifestyle that is set to dominate the Western world in the 21st century. The diet has undergone harsh criticism, but there's no doubt it works for those who stick to it. Surely obesity is more dangerous? There's an awful lot of conflicting information out there, but one point nutritionists will agree on: if you eat less, you will lose weight.

To be true to this project, I went on a low-carb diet myself. I have been a normal, healthy weight for several years and don't have much weight to lose, but I have had plump phases in my life and I know how fabulous it feels to get thin. What I really wanted was to "live the low-carb life" to get a clearer picture of what the diet is really like. I was surprised! Almost immediately, I noticed that my appetite shrank. I was snacking less and eating smaller meals. I really did feel that my mind was more focused and I had sustained energy levels. I could sit at my desk for hours without even thinking about what I would wander into the kitchen to nibble on next. Unlike other diets, there was not a sense of deprivation or longing. After 2 weeks, my clothes felt loose and I had lost about 3 lbs. This proved to me that the diet works.

I think it's the stereotype of the "fat chef" that often prompts people to ask me, "How do you stay so slim?" My reply is always the same. "Plenty of exercise!" Whatever diet you're on, that's the key. I advise anyone embarking on a low-carb diet to read the books that are out there and decide what's right for them. Pair that up with increased physical exercise, and you can hardly fail to lose weight.

Developing these recipes was a whole new experience for me. I established a finite set of ingredients which were low-carb and vegetarian. Within that realm, I applied the same passion and relish as I always do, aiming to create the most sumptuous dishes I could muster. I hope this cookbook will contribute some ideas to your repertoire, vegetarian or not, low-carb or not, and that the recipes are as fun to cook as they are to eat. It's good food—enjoy!

Celia x

Celia Brooks Brown, May 2004

# how it works

There are 2 factors that make the low-carb diet unique:

The first is insulin control. When you eat carbohydrates, the body quickly converts them into the basic sugars they are composed of. The presence of these sugars in the bloodstream gives you a surge of energy, but also triggers the pancreas to produce insulin. Insulin's job is to enter the bloodstream and remove the sugars for storage as fat. This happens fast, and once the insulin has stored the sugars, your appetite returns. So it follows that if you eat fewer carbs, your body doesn't have the sugars there to burn for fuel, so it resorts to the fat stores already there, and off drops the excess weight.

The second factor is how protein affects appetite. Carbs burn up quickly; protein takes longer to digest. So a high protein meal, with plenty of tofu or eggs, for example, will leave you feeling fuller for longer. You are then less likely to snack between meals and end up eating less overall. If you do fancy a snack, you'll get more mileage out of a high protein one.

Protein is the obvious stumbling block for a vegetarian on a low-carb diet. It is assumed that the diet is too limiting without meat or fish. While it would be impossible to follow a no-carb diet as a veggie (and would be seriously discouraged from a health point of view), there are actually plenty of high-protein, low-carb options available, especially eggs and tofu, and they both dominate the recipes in this book. Because of the high vegetable content of many of the recipes, I would argue that going low-carb vegetarian could be one of the healthiest diets around. After all, vegetables are the elixir of life, and these recipes provide many ways to get your recommended 5 portions-a-day (see also the "fresh produce" section, *page 15*).

## protein

Protein is your best friend on a low-carb diet. Many vegetarian protein sources, except nuts and cheese, are also low in fat, which increases your chances of successful weight loss. Not only that, but all natural vegetarian protein sources are rich in other nutrients which can improve your general health. Beans and legumes are protein-rich, but they are also carb-rich. A diet such as Atkins® with an "induction" phase of extreme carb reduction does not permit them, but they are a healthy type of carb which should be reintroduced into the diet at a later phase.

### eggs

Eggs are often referred to as "the perfect protein." As with all other animal protein sources, they contain all 20 amino acids which form a complete protein, all wrapped up in a neat little shell. Eggs contain many beneficial minerals and vitamins, including vitamin E—a natural antioxidant which helps prevent disease. The only down-side to eggs is the cholesterol in the yolk. For this reason, nutritionists recommend that you don't exceed 7 eggs per week.

I can't stress enough the importance of buying organic eggs. Not only do organic chickens have a happier life in their free–range surroundings, but their diet is totally vegetarian and free of chemicals, antibiotics and hormones. On a low-carb diet your egg intake will be high. Since what goes into the chicken goes into the egg, which then goes into you, organic is the only way to go. Yes, they are a little bit more expensive, but only by a fraction, well worth spending.

## soy

The mighty soybean is Nature's gift to vegetarians. It is one of the only plant sources of complete protein (as with animal protein, it too contains all 20 amino acids). Soybean products are low in fat and carbs, high in protein and disease-preventing antioxidants, and also high in plant estrogens which have many benefits, including reducing the risk of breast cancer. In fact, the USFDA recommends that everyone incorporate at least 25 g soy protein into their daily diet, to help reduce cholesterol levels. While most natural foods lose their good qualities and nutrients in processing, the opposite is true of soy. A cake of processed tofu has more concentrated nutrients than the raw bean, and fewer carbs weight for weight.

As with eggs, organic soy is best. Be aware that non-organic soy is probably genetically modified.

## nuts

Nuts and seeds are little powerhouses of nutrition. They are high in protein and also boast a high vitamin E, fibre and mineral content. Brazil nuts contain high levels of selenium, which is particularly beneficial for vegetarians as it's one of the only plant sources of this essential mineral. Nuts score high in the fat department, but it's good, unsaturated fat. Walnuts are one of the only plant sources of omega-3 fats, the cholesterol-lowering fats found in oily fish.

## dairy

The important thing to remember here is that dairy products, especially cheese, contain harmful saturated fat. There are many low-fat dairy products available, but they almost always contain a higher carb count. ½ cup/3½ fl oz/100 g of low-fat yogurt contains 7.4 g carbs, while ½ cup/3½ fl oz/100 g of thick and creamy Greek-style (strained plain) yogurt contains just 4.8 g. As a general rule of thumb, the higher the fat content of the dairy item, the lower the carbs—butter and most cheeses contain none. All dairy foods are products—they have been processed by manufacturers—so always check the nutritional information on the packaging, in case some extra carbs have sneaked in.

# fiber

One criticism by nutritionists of low-carb diets is the lack of fiber, which is essential to keep the digestive system on track. A vegetarian low-carb diet is safe from this worry, provided you eat plenty of the permitted low-carb vegetables used in this book.

# sugar

This one is the BIG no-no. All types of sugar, refined or not, are pure carbohydrate and will send your insulin levels soaring and throw your metabolism off kilter if you are maintaining a strict low-carb lifestyle.

Low-calorie sweetener is the low-carb alternative. All recipes in this book which contain a sweet element were developed using Splenda® brand granular sweetener (see www.splenda.com for more information). This product is sucralose, which is actually made from sugar, but has a concentrated sweet flavor, so you can use less. Unlike other sweeteners such as aspartame (NutraSweet®), it is suitable for cooking and will stay sweet when subjected to heat. It does have a bit of an aftertaste, but it seems to taste more authentic when an acidic element such as lemon is introduced. This is also true of other sweeteners—have you ever noticed how much a squeeze of lemon improves the flavor of diet cola?

# fat

Fats, like carbs, are often misunderstood—it is a blanket generalisation to assume they are all bad. Actually, there are good fats and bad fats. It can be boiled down simply: animal sources of fat, including eggs and dairy, are bad fats (with the exception of oily fish). Plant sources are good fats. Good fats—monounsaturated, polyunsaturated and omega 3—are an essential part of our diet and actually lower cholesterol. Bad fats are saturated fats which raise cholesterol levels and clog the arteries. The worst offenders are trans fats—highly processed solid fats used in manufacturing, which have been proven dangerous. Always check labels on processed foods and avoid anything that contains the word "hydrogenated" in the ingredients.

Fat contains twice the calories of carbs, so it seems logical that if you cut out fat, you'll lose calories and hence weight, but this is a misconception which led to an obsession with avoiding fat. As with carbs, the trick is actually to avoid the bad and enjoy the good, and as with all things, in moderation. Not all the recipes in this book are free of saturated fats. Take three recipes as a case in point: Eggs Florentine (*page 22*), Spinach and Ricotta Gnocchi with Sage Butter (*page 63*) and Chocolate Marzipan Cheesecake (*page 115*) all contain rather a lot of butter, which sends saturated fat levels sky-high. They all taste heavenly though, so enjoy them occasionally and avoid other saturated fats on the days you eat them—that is, if you have Eggs Florentine for breakfast, it's best not to have the other two for lunch!

# carbs

Not all carbs are your enemy. There are evil carbs and angelic ones. Generally, the bad guys are the white, refined carbs: white bread, white pasta, potatoes, white rice and white sugar. These are the foods that will give you a surge of energy followed by a crash and a new wave of hunger pangs, potentially leading to progressive munching, bingeing and weight gain. To make matters worse, they have few nutritional benefits otherwise. The good guys are the unrefined carbs: whole grains, including brown rice, wholemeal pasta, fruits and vegetables. These are essential for a healthy diet. Hard-core low-carbers following Atkins® will forego all grains, most fruits and some vegetables for the initial "induction" weight-loss stage. This book is suitable for people in that phase of the diet, and will be beneficial for every phase of the diet, as a supplement to reintroducing the good carbs in later stages.

# The last word... water

Drinking water is one of the most important parts of weight loss and daily function generally. It flushes out toxins, gives a feeling of fullness, speeds up weight loss and keeps every cell in your body functioning properly. Keep a bottle with you at all times and drink at least 8 glasses (3½ pints/2 liters) a day.

# essential guidelines for a healthy low-carb diet

- Eat the right carbs: plenty of permitted vegetables and wholefoods. Avoid refined carbs and sugars.

- Increase your lean protein intake. At each meal, make the protein portion the larger one, the carb portion the smaller one, and always include fresh vegetables.

- As well as eating your greens, take a multivitamin and mineral supplement.

- Avoid too much saturated fat. Treat yourself to sat-fat splurges only occasionally.

- Relax and enjoy cooking. Bon appetit!

# the low-carb kitchen

If you are committing to a low-carb diet, especially one that requires a very limiting "induction" phase, then it's a good idea to have a "carb cull" and remove all temptation from your kitchen. Gather all high-carb foods and give to friends or donate them to charity. If other members of your household are still eating carbs, then designate a "carb cupboard" for them and stash their ingredients away; out of sight, out of mind.

Outlined here is a selection of foods which are acceptable on the diet. Keeping a well-stocked kitchen will make the diet easy to follow and the cooking more enjoyable. In the case of fresh produce, do try to buy what's in season close to the time you want to cook it, and buy organic where possible.

## * = read the label

Products containing sugar, corn syrup, modified starch, and anything hydrogenated should be avoided.

## eggs

- Up to 7 a week per person
- Buy organic
- Store in the fridge

## tofu

- Firm—store in the fridge. Unused portions can be stored covered in fresh water in the fridge for up to 3 days, changing the water daily. Can be frozen
- Silken—usually sold in a long-life carton. Unused portions should be stored in the fridge and used within 24 hours
- Smoked—store in the fridge. Can be frozen
- Flavored*/marinated*—store in the fridge. Can be frozen

# other soy/vegetarian products, dried, chilled or frozen

- Soy flour (defatted)—store in the fridge
- Textured vegetable protein (TVP)*
- Vegetarian ground meat substitute*
- Quorn™ and Quorn™ products*
- Yves® products*
- Vegetarian hot dogs*, sausages*
- Soy bacon bits* and strips*
- Vegetarian deli meat such as sliced "ham" and "chicken"*

# dairy

- Cheese, cream cheese
- Cottage cheese
- Ricotta, mascarpone
- Butter
- Sour cream
- Whipping cream
- Semi-skimmed milk
- Thick/Greek (strained plain)/low-fat yogurt

# nuts/seeds

- All types. Store in airtight container in a cool place for a short period, or in the freezer for longer periods. Cashew nuts are the only relatively high-carb nuts, but fine in moderation

# spices

- All types. Store away from sunlight. Buy whole spices and grind fresh if possible. Check the label of certain spice mixtures which might contain sugar

# condiments/flavorings

- Splenda® low-calorie sweetener
- Sea salt crystals
- Almond essence*
- Pure vanilla essence*
- Tabasco
- Other chili sauces*
- Soy sauce, light and dark
- Mustard*
- Mayonnaise*
- Peanut butter*
- Cooking wines: sherry, Madeira, Marsala

# cans/jars

- Italian chopped tomatoes
- Artichoke hearts/bottoms
- Pickled vegetables*
- Pickled chilis such as jalapeños*
- Green and black olives
- Capers
- Roasted bell peppers*
- Water chestnuts
- Palm hearts
- Coconut milk/cream
- Pesto*
- Tapenade*

# fresh produce

- All green vegetables and salad
- Cauliflower
- Green onions, shallots, onions, garlic, leeks
- Eggplant
- Pumpkin
- Asparagus
- Zucchini
- Celery root, rutabaga, turnips
- Bell peppers
- Mung bean sprouts and other sprouted seeds such as alfalfa
- Avocados
- Cucumber
- Celery
- Fennel
- Green beans, snow peas, sugar snaps
- Mushrooms of all types, fresh and dried
- Radishes
- Tomatoes
- Red and green chilis
- Ginger
- Lemons, limes
- Fresh berries, melon

# drinks

- Natural mineral water—drink 8 glasses (3½ pints/2 liters) a day
- Herbal tea (sweetened with artificial sweetener only)
- Tea/coffee
- White wine
- Vodka and some other spirits*
- Sugar-free mixers/carbonated drinks*

# 01: breakfast

A high-protein fuel injection at breakfast will rocket-propel you into a sustained orbit until lunchtime. Breakfast is the key to keeping hunger at bay throughout the day. Don't miss it...

# blueberry almond griddle cakes

**These southern-style pancakes are sweet, nutty and laced with bursting blueberries. Don't be confused by putting the berries in the pan before the batter—it is the best way to distribute and cook them evenly, rather than mixing them into the batter.**

6 tbsp soy flour
4 tbsp ground almonds
2 tbsp sweetener
½ tsp baking powder
pinch of salt
2 eggs
¼ cup/2 fl oz/50 ml heavy
   or whipping cream
2 tsp butter
¾ cup/3 oz/75 g blueberries
2 tbsp Greek (strained plain)
   yogurt, to serve (optional)

Makes 12/Serves 4

Preheat the oven to 250°F/120°C for keeping the griddle cakes warm. Place soy flour, almonds, sweetener, baking powder, salt, eggs, and cream in a blender and process until smooth.

Heat a large non-stick pan or griddle over a low to medium flame and add 1 tsp of the butter. Tilt the pan to coat the surface with the melted butter. Allowing 4–5 blueberries for each griddle cake, place a cluster of berries in three places in the pan and carefully pour the batter over them to make three griddle cakes about 2½ inches in diameter. Cook until risen, golden on the undersides and dry around the edges, then flip over and cook the other sides until golden. Keep warm in the oven while you cook the remaining batches, adding the remaining butter between batches. Serve warm with the yogurt, if you like.

**per serving**
**carbs: 5 g  protein: 11 g  calories: 267  fiber: 3 g  fat: 23 g (saturated fat: 8 g)**

# melon berry power smoothie

**Blast off with this fruity, high-protein concoction—guaranteed to give your day a kick start.**

5 oz/150 g silken tofu
½ cup/2 oz/50 g cantaloupe
   melon chunks
⅓ cup/2 oz/50 g raspberries
3 tbsp ground almonds
½ tsp almond extract
1 tsp apple pie spice
2 tbsp sweetener, or to taste
5 tbsp water

Serves 2

Place all ingredients in a blender and process until smooth. Taste for sweetness and add more sweetener to suit.

**per serving**
**carbs: 7.5 g  protein: 11 g  calories: 217  fibre: 3 g  fat: 16 g (saturated fat: 1.5 g)**

Illustrated on page 65.

# chocolate breakfast shake

**Chocolate for breakfast? Why not? Unsweetened cocoa powder contains beneficial antioxidants, you get a little pro-biotic culture from the yogurt, and tofu is loaded with protein, so this delicious sugar-free shake is healthier than you might think.**

5 oz/150 g silken tofu
2 tbsp Greek (strained
   plain) yogurt
1 cup/7 fl oz/200 ml water
2 tbsp unsweetened
   cocoa powder
½ tsp pure vanilla extract
½ tsp ground cinnamon
3 tbsp sweetener, or to taste

Serves 2

Place all ingredients in a blender and process until smooth. Taste for sweetness and add more sweetener to suit. For a thicker texture, use less water in the mixture.

**per serving**
**carbs: 2 g  protein: 7 g  calories: 78  fiber: 0.5 g  fat: 5 g (saturated fat: 1.5 g)**

# japanese omelet

**Making this light, multi-layered, rolled omelet might take a little practice, but the result is mightily impressive. As you are making it, don't worry if some of the layers break up slightly, as they will repair themselves in the final step. The added mushrooms give the omelet a rich nutty flavor, but they are not essential. Can be made up to 1 hour in advance.**

**6 shiitake mushrooms**
**1 tbsp vegetable oil**
**8 organic eggs**
**½ cup/4 fl oz/120 ml Vegetable Stock (see page 128)**
**1 tbsp light soy sauce**

Serves 4

Discard the stems of the shiitake mushrooms and slice very thinly. Heat a large non-stick pan over a medium heat and add 2 tsp of the oil. Cook the mushrooms until they are tinged with gold, then drain on paper towels.

Beat the eggs with remaining ingredients in a jug. Reheat the pan with the remaining oil over a low to medium heat and pour in just enough of the egg mixture to cover the base, swirling to coat. Sprinkle with a few mushrooms. Cook until barely set but not dry, then loosen the edges with a spatula and fold over three or four times to one side of the pan. (It may help to use a wide fish slice, two spatulas or chopsticks.)

Pour in a little more egg mixture, swirl to coat the pan and allow the mixture to attach itself to the cooked omelet. Sprinkle on a few mushrooms and cook until barely set. Loosen as before and roll up in the opposite direction, starting with the previously cooked omelet.

Pour in more egg and mushrooms and repeat the process, back and forth, until the egg mixture is used up and you have a long "sausage" of omelet.

Spread out a large piece of foil. Slide the omelet into the middle and roll up in the foil, gently forming it into a firm brick shape. Keep warm until ready to serve, then unwrap on a board and cut into eight slices or four pieces.

**per serving**
**carbs: 0.3 g  protein: 16 g  calories: 216  fiber: 0.5 g  fat: 17 g (saturated fat: 4 g)**

# turkish breakfast

A satisfying, summery collection of tasty morsels, this traditional breakfast brings the essence of the Mediterranean to your table first thing in the morning. Boiling the egg in this fashion gives it a "buttery" yolk—not too runny, nor too powdery, but just right. This recipe serves one person, but you can multiply it any number of times. Strong black tea is the customary accompaniment.

1 organic egg
1 oz/25 g slice feta cheese
1 medium tomato,
   quartered
3 oz/75 g cucumber,
   thickly sliced
½ cup/2 oz/50 g good-
   quality black olives,
   such as Kalamata
1 tbsp olive oil
½ tsp dried oregano, or
   1 tsp fresh oregano
salt and freshly ground
   black pepper

Serves 1

Place the egg in a pan and cover with cold water. Bring to the boil, then simmer for 5 minutes. Drain and cool. Remove the shell and cut the egg in half—it should be set but the yolk should still be buttery. Place on a plate and add the feta, tomato, cucumber, and olives. Drizzle the olive oil over the mixture, sprinkle with oregano and season with salt and pepper.

per serving
carbs: 3 g   protein: 13 g   calories: 318   fiber: 2.5 g   fat: 28 g (saturated fat: 8 g)

# eggs florentine with broiled mushrooms

Juicy, truffle-scented portabello mushrooms replace English muffins in this timeless classic—a fabulous brunch dish. A little multitasking is required, but it's worth it. Warm plates are absolutely essential for serving—pop them in the base of the oven while the mushrooms are cooking. If you don't have a broiler, simply roast the mushrooms at 400°F/200°C instead.

4 organic eggs
4 large, flat portabello
   mushrooms
2 tbsp olive oil
2 tsp truffle oil (optional)
14 oz/400 g young
   spinach leaves
1 recipe Blender
   Hollandaise (see page 130)
salt and freshly ground
   black pepper

Serves 4

First, poach the eggs. Bring a ¾ inch depth of water to the boil in a large, non-stick skillet. Lower the heat to a gentle simmer. One at a time, carefully break each egg into a cup, then slide it into the water. Simmer for 2 minutes. Turn off the heat and leave the eggs to stand in the water for 10 minutes for slightly runny yolks. If you prefer a well-done yolk, return the pan to the heat for 1–2 minutes, until cooked to your liking. Place a couple of layers of paper towels on a plate. Remove the eggs from the pan with a slotted spatula and dry briefly on the paper.

Meanwhile, preheat the broiler to its highest setting. Snap the stems out of the mushrooms and discard. Brush the caps with olive oil and place, gill side up, on a cookie sheet. Season with salt and pepper and drizzle the remaining olive oil and truffle oil, if using, over the gills. Place under the broiler for about 8 minutes, until juicy.

Place the spinach in a large, heatproof bowl and pour boiling water over it. Stir until wilted, then drain thoroughly in a sieve or colander, pressing out the excess moisture with a potato masher. Keep the spinach warm while you make the hollandaise sauce, which should be made just before serving.

Place a broiled mushroom cap on each of four warm plates. Top with spinach, then a poached egg. Finish with warm hollandaise sauce and a good grinding of black pepper.

per serving
carbs: 2.5 g  protein: 14 g  calories: 499  fiber: 3 g  fat: 48 g (saturated fat: 23 g)

# kerala-style eggs

**My cooking is heavily influenced by India, partly because it's a vegetarian's paradise, but also because I have spent some time in Kerala, the southern-most state. This is my version of *"kitchri,"* one of my favourite Keralan breakfast dishes.**

4 organic eggs
1 tbsp peanut or
  sunflower oil
½ tsp black mustard seeds
2 green onions, chopped
1 fresh red chili, sliced or
  chopped (deseeded
  if large)
½ tsp finely grated fresh
  ginger
½ tsp ground turmeric
1 tomato, about
  3½ oz/100 g, chopped
handful of cilantro,
  chopped
salt and freshly ground
  black pepper
2 tsp Greek (strained plain)
  yogurt, to serve (optional)

Serves 2

Beat the eggs in a bowl with a pinch of salt until frothy. Set aside.

Heat a non-stick skillet over a medium to high heat and pour in the oil. Add the mustard seeds and when they start to pop, lower the heat. Add the green onions and chili and cook for about 1 minute, until fragrant. Add the ginger and turmeric and stir, then add tomatoes and cook for about 1 minute more.

When the tomatoes are heated through, pour in the eggs. When the eggs have set on the base of the pan, start stirring gently with a folding motion. Cook until nearly set, then stir in the cilantro and remove from the heat. Serve on warm plates with a spoonful of yogurt and plenty of freshly ground black pepper.

per serving
carbs: 2.5 g  protein: 16 g  calories: 240  fiber: 0.7 g  fat: 19 g (saturated fat: 5 g)

# three-minute egg and mushroom bowl

**The microwave is brilliant for cooking vegetables with a high water content such as mushrooms. Invented by my husband Daniel, this recipe is so speedy it must be the fastest low-carb breakfast in the West! The recipe is for one, but of course it can be multiplied—although it's best to cook each portion individually.**

1 large flat portabello
   mushroom, stem removed
1 tsp truffle oil or olive oil
1 egg
sea salt and freshly ground
   black pepper
1 oz/25 g Cheddar or
   Gruyère cheese, cut into
   2 slices
1 tsp bacon flavor soy
   bits (optional)

Serves 1

Choose a microwave-safe bowl that is just wide enough to accommodate the mushroom cap but not much bigger. Place the mushroom cap, gill side up, in the bowl. Drizzle the truffle oil or olive oil over the gills and season with salt and pepper. (You could also add a little chopped garlic or fresh herbs at this stage.)

Break the egg into the mushroom. Season lightly and prick the yolk with a fork to prevent it from exploding. Cross the cheese slices on top. Sprinkle over the bacon flavor soy bits, if using.

Microwave on high for 1 minute, then check. The cooking time is variable (1½–2 minutes), depending on the moisture content and size of the mushroom, the size of the egg, the power of the microwave, etc. It's best to judge by the cheese, which should be bubbly and slightly crisp. The egg white should be completely set.

**per serving**
**carbs: 0.2 g  protein: 15 g  calories: 223  fiber: 0.4 g  fat: 18 g (saturated fat: 8 g)**

# cottage cheese scramble

**This recipe produces the tastiest and easiest scrambled eggs, all done in just three minutes. The wonderful cottage cheese imparts a richness and texture that makes toast just seem irrelevant. You can supplement this breakfast with a veggie sausage or two (low-carb ones, of course—always read the label), cooked in the microwave for speed and ease.**

**4 eggs**
**4 tbsp cottage cheese,**
   **drained**
**sea salt and freshly ground**
   **black pepper**
**1 tsp butter**

Serves 2

Whisk together the eggs, cottage cheese, and seasoning in a bowl. Heat a non-stick skillet over a low heat and add the butter. Pour in the eggs. Cook until the underside is just set, then stir gently until the whole mixture is just set. Serve immediately.

(This can also be cooked in a microwave: Place the egg mixture in a microwave-safe bowl and add the butter. Cook on high power for 1 minute, then stir. Cook for a further 1–2 minutes, stopping and stirring with a clean fork every minute until cooked to your liking.)

**per serving**
**carbs: 1 g  protein: 19 g  calories: 228  fiber: 0 g  fat: 17 g (saturated fat: 6 g)**

# cottage cheese pancakes with berry purée

**A short-stack of these classic American-style pancakes makes a filling breakfast. They can also be frozen (after cooking and cooling), then reheated in a toaster straight from the freezer.**

**2 tbsp soy flour
1 tsp sweetener
½ cup/3½ oz/100 g cottage cheese
2 eggs, beaten
½ tsp baking powder
generous pinch of sea salt
1 tsp sunflower oil
Raspberry Purée (see page 131), to serve**

Serves 2

Preheat the oven to about 250°F/120°C to keep the pancakes warm once cooked.

Beat together the flour, sweetener, cottage cheese, eggs, baking powder, and salt until well mixed, making sure there are no lumps of flour.

Heat a large non-stick skillet over a medium heat and add the oil. Cook tablespoonfuls of the mixture in batches. When golden underneath, flip the pancakes over carefully—they remain slightly runnier on top than standard pancakes. Cook the second side, then remove to a plate and keep warm while you cook another batch.

Serve warm with Raspberry Purée spooned on top of each pancake.

**per serving
carbs: 5 g  protein: 17 g  calories: 194  fiber: 2 g  fat: 12 g (saturated fat: 3.5 g)**

# almond muffins

These protein-packed muffins are easy to grab and eat on busy mornings. This recipe makes a large batch, but they keep well for up to four days in an airtight container or can be frozen. Alternatively, you can divide the recipe in half or into thirds, if you want to make less.

**For the dry mixture**
2 cups/8 oz/225 g soy flour
1¼ cups/5 oz/150 g ground
 almonds
3 tsp baking powder
15 tbsp sweetener
1 tsp salt

**For the wet mixture**
6 eggs, beaten
1 cup/4½ fl oz/135 ml
 reduced-fat sour cream
1 tbsp vanilla extract
1½ tsp almond extract
½ cup/4½ fl oz/135 ml
 sunflower oil

**To decorate and serve**
36 blanched almonds
butter

Makes 12

Preheat oven to 350°F/180°C. Grease a 12-cup muffin pan or line with paper cases and set aside.

Combine all the dry ingredients in a bowl, smoothing out any lumps in the flour.

Beat together all the wet ingredients in another bowl. Thoroughly combine the two mixtures, but do not over-mix.

Pour the batter into the prepared muffin pan. Place 3 blanched almonds on top of each. Bake for 20–30 minutes, until risen, golden and firm. Rest for 5 minutes in the pan, then turn out onto a wire rack. Serve warm, with butter for spreading.

per serving
carbs: 6 g  protein: 14 g  calories: 298  fiber: 3 g  fat: 24 g (saturated fat: 4 g)

Illustrated on page 65.

# 02: small courses

These little dishes can be mixed and matched with other recipes from this book, for a table full of treats, the prelude to a main course, instalments in a multi-course feast, or served as a single light meal.

# asian wild mushroom broth

**Dried mushrooms such as shiitake have a concentrated flavor that is released into this light and cleansing broth, giving it a rich, nutty undertone.**

**4 cups/1¾ pints/1 litre Vegetable Stock (see page 128)**
**10 dried shiitake mushrooms or other dried mushrooms, about ¼ oz/10 g**
**1 tbsp sunflower oil**
**1 garlic clove, chopped**
**¾ inch piece of fresh ginger, chopped**
**3½ oz/100 g firm tofu, finely diced**
**2 cups/5 oz/150 g mixed wild mushrooms, especially enoki, shimeji, oyster, shiitake, cut into bite-size pieces**
**1 tbsp dark soy sauce**
**1 carton, about ¾ oz/20 g, alfalfa or mixed sprouts, trimmed and cleaned**

Serves 4

Place the stock and dried mushrooms in a saucepan and bring to the boil. Simmer for at least 15 minutes.

Meanwhile, heat a small skillet over a moderate flame and add the sunflower oil. Add garlic, ginger, and tofu and stir-fry for about 2 minutes, until fragrant but not brown. Add mushrooms and stir-fry until soft and juicy. Add the soy sauce and remove from the heat.

Empty the contents of the skillet into the simmering stock. Bring back to a simmer for 5 minutes, then taste for seasoning. Ladle into bowls, scatter alfalfa or mixed sprouts over the top and serve.

per serving
**carbs: 8 g  protein: 13 g  calories: 141  fiber: 0.5 g  fat: 7 g (saturated fat: 0.4 g)**

# egg flower soup

"Flower" in the title of this recipe refers to the appearance of the eggs, which resemble chrysanthemum petals as they cook in this delicious and healthy soup. The vegetables can be adapted according to what you have available—you can substitute spinach, watercress, asparagus, or zucchini, or add a little extra ginger or chili if you like.

1 tbsp sunflower oil
¾ cup/3½ oz/100 g green onions, chopped
2 tsp sesame seeds
1 cup/3½ oz/100 g broccoli, chopped
1 cup/3½ oz/100 g green cabbage, finely shredded
4 cups/1¾ pints/1 litre Vegetable Stock (see page 128)
1 tbsp rice vinegar
1 tsp Chinese five-spice powder
3 organic eggs
2 tbsp light soy sauce
1 tbsp dry sherry
sea salt and freshly ground black pepper

Serves 4

Heat a pan over a low to medium heat and add the oil. Add the green onions and sesame seeds and cook for about 2 minutes, until the sesame seeds start to turn golden. Add the broccoli and cabbage (or green vegetables of your choice) and stir-fry for about 1 minute, until bright green. Pour in the stock, season with pepper and add the vinegar and five-spice. Bring to the boil.

Meanwhile, beat together the eggs, soy sauce, and sherry in a jug. While stirring the boiling soup rapidly and constantly, gradually pour in the egg mixture in a steady stream. The eggs should set immediately and the soup is ready to serve.

per serving
carbs: 5 g  protein: 9 g  calories: 150  fiber: 2 g  fat: 10 g (saturated fat: 2 g)

# fragrant coconut broth

**Here's the closest thing you can possibly get to fresh coconut milk—an easy method of reconstituting dried coconut, then pressing out the milk. You'll be amazed how light and refreshing it tastes.**

3 cups/9 oz/250 g
  dry shredded coconut
5 cups/2 pints/1.25 liters
  boiling water
1½ inch piece of fresh
  ginger, peeled
2 lemon grass stalks,
  trimmed
2 tbsp light soy sauce, or
  to taste
1 tbsp sweetener
1 cup/2 oz/50 g white
  mushrooms, sliced
½ cup/2 oz/50 g broccoli
  florets, chopped
1 tbsp lemon juice
handful of cilantro leaves

Serves 4

Place the coconut in a bowl, pour over the boiling water and leave to cool. When cold, purée with a hand-held or upright blender, then push through a sieve, squeezing out as much coconut milk as possible; there should be just under 4 cups/1¾ pints/1 liter.

Slice the ginger and lemon grass—doing this now will maximize the flavor. Place in a pan with the coconut milk, soy sauce, and sweetener.

Bring to the boil, lower the heat and simmer, stirring occasionally, for 10 minutes. Add mushrooms and broccoli, return to the boil and cook for 3 minutes. Ladle the broth into small bowls. Season with a little lemon juice in each bowl, top with cilantro leaves and serve.

per serving
**carbs: 5 g  protein: 5 g  calories: 388  fiber: 9 g  fat: 39 g (saturated fat: 33 g)**

Illustrated on page 68.

# porcini mushroom soup with thyme

**Dried porcini mushrooms are a magic stock item with the power to transform the ordinary into something elegant. Cooking this velvety soup fills the house with delectable earthy aromas.**

½ cup/1 oz/25 g dried
   porcini mushrooms
2½ cups/1 pint/600 ml
   boiling Vegetable Stock
   (see page 128) or water
2 tbsp olive oil
3 garlic cloves, crushed
8 cups/1¼ lb/500 g flat or
   other mushrooms,
   coarsely chopped
1½ tsp salt
bunch of fresh thyme,
   rinsed and tied together,
   or 1 tsp dried thyme
⅔ cup/¼ pint/150 ml
   Madeira, sherry
   or Marsala
4 tbsp reduced-fat sour
   cream
4 tbsp chopped parsley
freshly ground black pepper

Serves 4

Rinse the porcini to remove any soil or grit, then place in a bowl and pour the boiling stock or water over them. Leave for 20 minutes, then strain over a bowl, reserving the liquid. Coarsely chop the porcini.

Heat the olive oil in a pan over a low to medium heat and add the garlic. Cook for just a few seconds, until it becomes fragrant, without letting it burn or color too much. Add the chopped mushrooms and porcini and season with the salt and plenty of pepper. Stir, then cover and cook, stirring occasionally, for about 10 minutes, until the mushrooms have collapsed and are stewing in their juices.

Add the thyme and wine, then carefully pour in the reserved mushroom soaking liquid, leaving behind any extra grit which may have settled. Bring to the boil, then lower the heat to a simmer. Cook, uncovered, for 10 minutes. Cool briefly, then remove and discard the thyme bundle, if using, and purée the soup with a hand-held blender or in a food processor. Check the seasoning. The texture of the soup may vary depending on how juicy your mushrooms are; if it seems too thick, dilute with a little boiling water. Ladle into bowls and finish each with a tablespoon of sour cream and chopped parsley.

**per serving**
**carbs: 7 g  protein: 4 g  calories: 163  fiber: 1.5 g  fat: 8 g (saturated fat: 2.5 g)**

# smoky eggplant timbales

"Timbale" describes anything prepared in a small, round mold, either layered, as here, or solid, as in Red Bell Pepper and Goat's Cheese Timbales (see opposite). Choose plump eggplants with about the same circumference as the ramekins, but remember that they shrink a lot when cooked. The smoky pesto has a dazzling flavor, and can be used as a sauce in other dishes (see Spaghetti Squash with Smoked Chili Pesto, page 58).

2 large eggplants, about
  1¼ lb/500 g total
2 garlic cloves, sliced
olive oil
½ cup/4 oz/125 g ricotta
  cheese
salt and freshly ground
  black pepper
1 cup/2 oz/50 g arugula
  leaves, to garnish

**For the smoky pesto**
1 tsp smoked paprika or
  pimentón
bunch of fresh basil
½ cup/2 oz/50 g pine nuts
1 garlic clove
⅓ cup/1 oz/25 g grated
  fresh Parmesan cheese
3 tbsp olive oil
pinch of salt

Serves 4

Preheat the oven to 375°F/190°C.

Slice the eggplants into ½ inch thick rounds. Mix the garlic with some olive oil in a cup and brush both sides of the rounds. Place on a cookie sheet and sprinkle the sliced garlic on top of them. Season with salt and pepper and bake for 20–30 minutes, until soft and barely golden. Leave to cool.

Make the pesto by processing all the ingredients in the food processor, adding the olive oil at the end. Taste for seasoning.

Brush 4 ramekins lightly with olive oil and place an eggplant round in each. Top with about a tablespoon of ricotta, a generous spoonful of pesto, then another eggplant round. Continue with another layer of ricotta, pesto, then eggplant. (Some pieces will be smaller than others, so use as many pieces of eggplant as necessary to fill the layer.)

Place the ramekins on a cookie sheet and bake for 15–20 minutes, until sizzling. Cool briefly before inverting. To do this, place a plate upside down on top of each timbale and flip over. Arrange arugula leaves around the timbales and serve.

**per serving**
**carbs: 5 g  protein: 16 g  calories: 541  fiber: 3 g  fat: 51 g (saturated fat: 11 g)**

# red bell pepper and goat's cheese timbales

**Very elegant, coral-colored custards with a velvety texture, these can be eaten warm or cold with a small salad of young leaves. Team up with Avocado and Lemon Salad (see page 104) for an exquisite light lunch.**

**2 red bell peppers, about 11½ oz/325 g trimmed weight, halved and cored**
**11 oz/300 g mild, rindless soft goat's cheese**
**1 garlic clove, crushed with salt in a mortar or with a garlic crusher**
**2 organic eggs**
**generous grinding of nutmeg**
**butter, for greasing**
**salt and freshly ground black pepper**

Serves 4

Preheat the broiler or oven to its highest setting. Place the bell peppers, cut side down, on a cookie sheet and broil or roast until the skins are blackened and charred all over. Transfer to a plastic bag, tie the top and leave to sweat until cool, then peel off the skins.

Preheat the oven to 300°F/150°C. Place the roasted bell peppers, goat's cheese, and garlic in a food processor and process until smooth. Season to taste. Add the eggs, one at a time, and a good grinding of nutmeg. Process until absolutely smooth.

Generously grease four ramekins with butter and place in a roasting pan or ovenproof dish. Divide the mixture among the ramekins. Pour boiling water into the roasting pan or dish to come halfway up the sides of the ramekins. Bake for 30 minutes, until firm. Remove from the oven and place the timbales on an oven rack to cool slightly, then turn out onto plates (see method opposite) and serve.

Alternatively, leave to cool and serve chilled. To loosen from the ramekins, first stand in a bowl of hot water, then turn out.

**per serving**
**carbs: 6 g  protein: 21 g  calories: 310  fiber: 1 g  fat: 23 g (saturated fat: 14 g)**

Illustrated on page 66.

# halloumi-stuffed bell peppers

**Here's one of my favorite ways to stuff bell peppers with no fuss. The recipe is very easy to multiply if you're feeding a crowd. These make a good partner for Roasted Eggplant with Dill Sauce (see page 105). Use feta cheese if Halloumi is unavailable.**

2 red bell peppers
4 basil leaves
1 large garlic clove, sliced
1 tbsp pine nuts
2½ oz/75 g Halloumi cheese,
  sliced into 4 pieces
  (use feta if Halloumi
  is unavailable)
4 tbsp olive oil

Serves 2 or
  4 as an accompaniment

Preheat the oven to 400°F/200°C.

Cut the bell peppers in half from stem to base and de-seed but leave the stems intact. Place, skin side down, on a cookie sheet. Place a basil leaf in each bell pepper half, sprinkle with garlic and pine nuts, top with a slice of Halloumi, and finish with a tablespoon of olive oil in each bell pepper half.

Bake for 20–30 minutes, until the cheese is golden.

**per serving**
**carbs: 4 g  protein: 4 g  calories: 195  fiber: 1.25 g  fat: 17 g (saturated fat: 4.5 g)**

# portabello mushrooms with blue cheese custard

**These juicy little numbers will appreciate the company of a crisp lettuce salad such as romaine and oak leaf dressed with just a drop of white wine vinegar. Alternatively, turn them into a main course, paired up with Pumpkin and Rutabaga Mash (see page 108).**

6 large portabello
   mushrooms, about
   12 oz/340 g, stems
   removed
2 tbsp olive oil
2 garlic cloves, chopped
sea salt and freshly ground
   black pepper

**For the blue cheese
   custard**
3 oz/75 g blue cheese,
   such as Stilton, Roquefort
   or Gorgonzola, crumbled
⅔ cup/¼ pint/150 ml sour
   cream
2 organic egg yolks
1 tbsp finely chopped fresh
   tarragon leaves,
   plus extra to garnish

Serves 6

Preheat the oven to 350°F/180°C. Brush the mushroom caps with half the oil and place, gill side up, in an ovenproof dish just large enough to hold them in a single layer. Sprinkle the garlic over the gills, drizzle with the remaining oil and season with salt and pepper.

Beat together the cheese, sour cream, egg yolks, and tarragon with a pinch of salt. Spoon the mixture into the mushroom caps. Bake for about 20 minutes, until the custard is set and bubbly and the mushrooms are soft. Sprinkle more chopped tarragon over the mushrooms and serve.

per serving
**carbs: 1 g  protein: 6 g  calories: 207  fiber: 0.7 g  fat: 20 g (saturated fat: 11 g)**

# eggplant rarebit

**This is a filling, warming taste of cheese heaven!**

1 large eggplant, sliced
   into 8 rounds
1 tbsp olive oil, plus extra
   for greasing and brushing
4 shallots or 1 medium
   onion, sliced
5 tbsp white wine
1 cup/3½ oz/100 g
   grated Cheddar or
   Gruyère cheese
1 tsp dry mustard
2 organic eggs, beaten
salt and freshly ground
   black pepper

Serves 4

Preheat the oven to 375°F/190°C.

Brush each eggplant round all over with olive oil and place on a cookie sheet. Season with salt and pepper, and bake for 20–30 minutes, until softened and barely golden.

Preheat the broiler to its highest setting. Alternatively, increase the oven temperature to 425°F/220°C.

Heat a heavy pan over a medium heat, add the olive oil and cook the shallots or onion until softened. Turn the heat down as low as possible and add the wine, cheese, and mustard to the pan, stirring until the cheese melts. Add the beaten eggs and stir until the mixture thickens slightly, but remove from the heat before the eggs scramble. Spoon the mixture on to the baked eggplant and broil or bake until puffed and patched with gold. Grind over some black pepper and serve.

**per serving**
**carbs: 3 g  protein: 11 g  calories: 200  fiber: 2 g  fat: 15 g (saturated fat: 7 g)**

# spiced charred eggplants

**In this unusual cooking method, the eggplants steam in an aromatic broth which reduces to a thick glaze, and finally becomes a slightly charred crust. You will need a large, non-stick skillet for this. Just remember—don't stir. Serve with salad or cooked spinach.**

**2 medium eggplants, about
  1 lb 5 oz/600 g, cut into
  1 inch dice
2 tsp coriander seeds,
  lightly crushed
1 tsp cumin seeds
½ tsp ground turmeric
1 tsp salt
1 large green chili, cut into
  3–4 pieces
large handful of cilantro,
  chopped
1 cup/8 fl oz/250 ml water
¼ cup/2 oz/50 g butter,
  diced
freshly ground black pepper**

Serves 4

Arrange the eggplants in an even layer in a large, non-stick skillet. Sprinkle evenly with the coriander seeds, cumin seeds, turmeric, salt, chili, and chopped cilantro, and season with pepper. Pour in the water and dot with butter. Cover the pan, place over a high heat and bring to the boil. Shake the pan a few times and lower the heat to a simmer. Cook, covered and without stirring, for about 20 minutes, checking occasionally that the water has not dried out—if it has, add a little more.

After 20 minutes, the eggplants should be buttery soft and the liquid should have reduced to a thick glaze. Do not stir. Remove the lid and increase the heat. Reduce the sauce until it just starts to form a crust on the base of the pan. Remove from the heat.

Leave to stand for 2 minutes, then stir the crust through the eggplants. Serve hot or cold.

**per serving
carbs: 3.5 g  protein: 1.5 g  calories: 116  fiber: 3 g  fat: 11 g (saturated fat: 7 g)**

# 03: light lunch

Hearty soups and main-event salads feature here, perfect for a midday refuelling. Don't just restrict them to lunch—hot soups are perfect for winter nights, cool salads for balmy evenings…

# egg and avocado caesar

**I call this "Caesar" because of the sharp, eggy dressing that gives it a resemblance to the classic salad. Avocado and olives make it a well-rounded and substantial lunch or supper.**

6 organic eggs
4 tbsp freshly grated
   Parmesan cheese
4 tbsp white wine vinegar
1 tsp vegetarian
   Worcestershire sauce or
   light soy sauce
a small handful of fresh
   chives, snipped
4 tbsp olive oil
2 ripe avocados
juice of ½ lemon
2 hearts of romaine lettuce,
   torn
1 cup/3½ oz/100 g
   good-quality black olives,
   such as Kalamata
salt and freshly ground
   black pepper

Serves 4

Place the eggs in a small pan of cold water and bring to the boil. Boil for 5 minutes, then drain and rinse under cold water until cool. Shell and rinse again.

To make the dressing, place 2 shelled eggs in a bowl and mash well with a fork. Add the Parmesan, vinegar, Worcestershire or soy sauce, and chives, season with salt and pepper and whisk thoroughly. Gradually whisk in the oil.

Quarter the remaining eggs. Just before serving, peel, pit and quarter the avocados and sprinkle lightly with lemon juice to prevent discoloration. Make a bed of lettuce on each plate and top with avocados, egg quarters, and olives. Spoon the dressing over the salad.

**per serving**
**carbs: 2 g  protein: 20 g  calories: 480  fiber: 3.5 g  fat: 43 g (saturated fat: 11 g)**

# curried celery root soup with cilantro oil

**Thank heaven for celery root, one of the few low-carb root vegetables. It gives this soup a creamy and satisfying texture. Whole spices always produce the best flavor, but you can use ground spices instead if you're feeling lazy.**

**2 tsp coriander seeds**
**1 tsp cumin seeds**
**½ tsp chili flakes**
**1 oz/25 g/2 tbsp butter**
**2 tsp ground turmeric**
**1 large onion, chopped**
**3 garlic cloves, chopped**
**1 inch piece of fresh ginger, chopped**
**4 tbsp ground almonds**
**1 lb 10 oz/750 g celery root, diced**
**5 cups/2 pints/1.2 liters Vegetable Stock (see** *page 128*)
**salt and freshly ground black pepper**

**For the cilantro oil**
**1 small garlic clove**
**½ tsp coarse sea salt**
**handful of cilantro leaves**
**4 tbsp olive oil**

**4 tbsp heavy or whipping cream, to serve**

Serves 6

To make the soup, grind together the coriander seeds, cumin seeds, and chili flakes in a spice grinder or pound in a mortar with a pestle. Melt the butter in a pan over a low heat. Add the crushed spices and the turmeric and cook for about 1 minute, until fragrant. Add the onion, cover and cook for about 5 minutes, until translucent. Add the garlic, ginger, and almonds and cook for 1 minute. Add the celery root and stock and bring to the boil. Simmer for 20 minutes, until the celery root is tender, then purée the soup with a hand-held blender or food processor until smooth. Season to taste with salt and pepper.

To make the cilantro oil, grind all the ingredients together in a spice grinder or food processor, or pound to a smooth paste in a mortar with a pestle.

To serve, ladle the soup into bowls and garnish with the cilantro oil and cream. Sesame and Black Pepper Crispbreads (see *page 89*) are a good companion to this dish.

per serving
carbs: 6 g  protein: 4.5 g  calories: 237  fiber: 6 g  fat: 21 g (saturated fat: 7 g)

Illustrated on *page 67*.

# cauliflower, coconut and cardamom soup

**A thick and substantial potage, where three C's come together to form a dazzling combo. Two equally appealing textures can be achieved with this soup—chunky or smooth.**

1 tbsp groundnut oil or
   sunflower oil
1¼ lb/500 g cauliflower,
   chopped
5 oz/150 g zucchini,
   chopped
2 garlic cloves, chopped
3 green onions (whites and
   clean greens), chopped
sea salt and freshly ground
   black pepper
½ tsp cardamom seed (from
   about 20 pods), ground or
   pounded in a mortar
   or spice grinder
a good grinding of nutmeg
1 cup/½ pint/250 ml
   coconut milk
1½ cups/⅔ pint/375 ml
   Vegetable Stock (see
   page 128)

Serves 4

Heat a lidded pot over a moderate flame and add oil. Add cauliflower, zucchini, garlic, and green onions with a sprinkling of salt, pepper, the cardamom, and nutmeg. Stir, cover and sweat for about 10 minutes, stirring from time to time.

Pour in the coconut milk and stock and bring to the boil. Simmer for 10 minutes, or until the cauliflower is meltingly tender. Cool slightly, then for a slightly chunky texture, use a potato masher to crush the soup. Alternatively, use a hand-blender to purée until smooth.

Serve with Sesame and Black Pepper Crispbreads (see *page 89*).

per serving
**carbs: 8 g  protein: 8 g  calories: 192  fiber: 3 g  fat: 15 g (saturated fat: 6 g)**

# tofu, mint and palm heart salad with hot and spicy dressing

**Mint, ginger, garlic, chili, and toasted sesame seeds all sing a lovely harmony in this multi-textural, clean-flavored salad. If palm hearts are not available, use canned water chestnuts.**

9 oz/250 g fresh firm tofu, drained, patted dry, and cut into ¾ inch cubes

1 recipe Sweet Chili Sauce (see *page 132*), made with green chilis

2 tbsp sesame seeds

2 tsp sesame oil

8 Chinese cabbage leaves, lower halves shredded, top halves left intact

small bunch of fresh mint, leaves stripped

1 x 14 oz/400 g can palm hearts, drained (8 oz/225 g drained weight), diagonally sliced

1 inch piece of fresh ginger, cut into slivers

Serves 4

Place the tofu in a shallow dish and pour the chili sauce over it. Leave to marinate at room temperature for 30 minutes or for longer in the refrigerator.

Heat a dry skillet over a medium heat and add sesame seeds. Cook, stirring occasionally, until golden and popping. Transfer to a small bowl and leave to cool.

Drain the tofu, reserving the sauce. Mix the sauce with the sesame oil, beating well.

To assemble the salad, arrange two leaf tops on each of four plates. Mix together the shredded leaves, mint, palm hearts, and ginger slivers, and divide among the plates. Top with marinated tofu and toasted sesame seeds. Spoon the dressing over each salad.

**per serving**
**carbs: 4 g  protein: 8.5 g  calories: 135  fiber: 1 g  fat: 8 g (saturated fat: 1 g)**

Illustrated on *page 68*.

# chinese-spice tofu and mesclun salad

**Tofu just needs a little loving attention to give it life. This simple treatment gives it masses of flavor, a light, crisp texture on the outside, and a creamy interior.**

1¼ lb/500 g firm tofu
4 tbsp sunflower oil
6 green onions, sliced
4 garlic cloves, sliced
1½ inch piece of fresh
   ginger, grated
2 tsp Chinese five-spice
   powder
4 tbsp dark soy sauce
2 tbsp rice vinegar
2 tbsp sweetener
7 oz/200 g mesclun greens
salt

Serves 4

Drain the tofu and wrap in paper towels. Set aside while you prepare the remaining ingredients.

When you are ready to cook, cut the tofu into 1 inch cubes. Heat the oil in a large, non-stick skillet over a medium heat and add the tofu, green onions, garlic, ginger, five-spice powder, and a pinch of salt. Stir-fry for about 3 minutes, until the tofu is light golden.

Add the soy sauce, vinegar, and sweetener. Heat through, then remove the pan from the heat. Transfer the mixture to a bowl and leave to cool.

Toss the cooled tofu mixture through the mesclun greens and serve immediately.

**per serving**
**carbs: 3 g  protein: 12 g  calories: 210  fiber: 0.7 g  fat: 17 g (saturated fat: 2 g)**

# warm exotic mushroom salad

I was lucky enough to be asked to present a short film for UKTV Food about a mushroom farm in Kent in southeast England. The farmer, Nigel Baddeley, is bravely growing exotic varieties from Japan in England for the first time: shimeji, nameko and eringii mushrooms, which all have a unique, nutty flavor. I created this recipe with the produce he gave me, but you could use any combination of wild or cultivated types, especially shiitake and oyster mushrooms.

2 tbsp/1 oz/25 g butter
2 garlic cloves, chopped
11 oz/300 g mixed wild and
   cultivated mushrooms,
   sliced if large
1 tsp fresh thyme leaves
½ cup/3½ fl oz/100 ml
   Madeira wine
⅓ cup/3 oz/75 g
   mascarpone cheese
2 small Bibb lettuces
sea salt and freshly ground
   black pepper

Serves 4

Melt the butter in a wide skillet over a low heat and cook the garlic until fragrant. Add the mushrooms, season with salt and pepper and cook gently until softened. Add the thyme and Madeira and cook for a further 2 minutes. Stir in mascarpone and cook until it coats the mushrooms. Remove the pan from the heat and cool briefly.

Arrange the lettuce leaves on plates and spoon the warm mushroom mixture over them. Serve immediately.

per serving
carbs: 1 g  protein: 2 g  calories: 171  fiber: 1 g  fat: 14 g (saturated fat: 9 g)

# warm poached egg salad with tarragon vinaigrette

**My good friend Jennifer Joyce has kindly let me use this recipe from her gorgeous book** *The Well-Dressed Salad*. **This sophisticated salad is fully appreciated, she insists, "with a glass of chilled white Burgundy." I couldn't agree more—and only 1 g carbohydrate per glass!**

4 organic eggs
1⅓ cups/7 oz/200 g green
   beans
1 tbsp olive oil
salt

**For the dressing**
2 tsp Dijon mustard
1 tsp red wine vinegar
½ tsp sea salt
¾ cup/6 fl oz/175 ml
   peanut oil
1 tbsp capers, rinsed and
   chopped
1 tbsp finely chopped flat
   leaf parsley
leaves from 2 tarragon
   sprigs, chopped
1 tbsp finely chopped
   shallot
freshly ground black pepper

Serves 4

First, poach the eggs. Bring a ¾ inch depth of water to the boil in a large, non-stick skillet. Reduce the heat to a low simmer. One at a time, carefully break each egg into a cup, then slide it into the water. Simmer for 2 minutes. Turn off the heat and let the eggs stand in the water for 10 minutes. They will then be perfectly cooked if you like the yolk slightly runny. If you prefer a well-done yolk, put the pan back on the heat for 1–2 minutes, until cooked to your liking. Place a couple of layers of paper towels on a plate. Remove the eggs from the pan with a slotted spatula and dry briefly on the paper.

Meanwhile, cook the beans and make the dressing. Bring a small pan of salted water to the boil. Blanch the beans for about 2 minutes, until tender but still firm. Drain and cool under cold running water or plunge into iced water to stop the cooking process.

To make the dressing, whisk together the mustard, vinegar, salt, and pepper to taste in a small bowl. Gradually whisk in the oil to emulsify. Stir in the capers, herbs, and shallot.

Return the beans to the dry pan and add the olive oil. Warm through over a medium heat. Place the warm beans on individual plates, top with an egg and spoon the dressing over them.

**per serving**
**carbs: 4 g  protein: 9 g  calories: 436  fiber: 1.5 g  fat: 42 g (saturated fat: 7 g)**

# cyprus salad

**Resembling its sister the Greek salad (also a low-carb choice), this salad uses Cyprus's unique cheese, Halloumi, instead of feta. If you can't find Halloumi, try slicing feta in the same way and broiling until golden on top.**

1 cup/3½ oz/100 g broccoli
   florets
half a cucumber, about
   5 oz/150 g, chopped
   into chunks
3 celery sticks, chopped
   into chunks
1 green bell pepper, cored
   and chopped into chunks
1 red bell pepper, cored
   and chopped into chunks
½ cup/2 oz/50 g good-
   quality black olives, such
   as Kalamata
handful of fresh flat leaf
   parsley, chopped
handful of fresh mint
   leaves, chopped
9 oz/250 g Halloumi cheese,
   sliced across the narrow
   end into 8 slices
juice of ½ a lemon

**For the dressing**
½ small red onion, chopped
2 tbsp fresh lemon juice
1 tsp fresh or dried thyme
4 tbsp extra virgin olive oil
sea salt and freshly ground
   black pepper

First make the dressing. Mix together the onion, lemon juice, and thyme and season with sea salt and pepper. Whisk in the olive oil, then taste and adjust the seasoning if necessary. Set aside for the flavors to mingle while you prepare the rest of the salad.

Boil, microwave or steam the broccoli florets for 3 minutes, until just tender. Refresh under cold running water, drain and pat dry.

Mix together the broccoli, cucumber, celery, bell peppers, olives, and herbs in a bowl.

When you are ready to serve, heat a large, non-stick skillet over a medium heat. Do not add oil. Arrange the Halloumi slices in the pan. Cook until golden underneath, then turn over and cook the other side. Meanwhile, stir the dressing through the salad and spoon onto plates.

As soon as the Halloumi is golden, squeeze the lemon juice over it in the hot pan and remove from the heat. Place the Halloumi on top of the salad and serve immediately.

per serving
**carbs: 8 g  protein: 12 g  calories: 311  fiber: 3 g  fat: 25 g (saturated fat: 10 g)**

Illustrated on *page 69*.

Serves 4

# teriyaki tofu
# with roasted broccoli

**Teriyaki is a rich and powerful Japanese flavor combination which brings out the best in tofu, and broccoli loves its company as well. Serve this with a few slices of cool cucumber to balance the salty-sweet flavor.**

½ cup/3½ fl oz/100 ml
   dark soy sauce
1 cup/7 fl oz/200 ml
   dry sherry
½ inch piece of fresh
   ginger, finely grated
7 oz/200 g firm tofu,
   patted dry and cut into
   2 triangles
4 tsp peanut or
   sunflower oil
1¾ cups/7 oz/200 g broccoli
   florets
cucumber slices, to serve
   (optional)

Serves 2

Preheat the oven to 400°F/200°C. Place the soy sauce, sherry and ginger in a small skillet and bring to the boil. Add the tofu and simmer for 5 minutes, then turn the tofu over and simmer for a further 5 minutes. Carefully lift the tofu from the hot sauce and place in a lightly oiled ovenproof dish. Reserve the sauce. Brush the top and sides of the tofu with 2 tsp oil.

Place the broccoli in a bowl and toss in the remaining oil. Arrange the broccoli around the tofu. Pour the reserved sauce over the broccoli and tofu. Roast for 25 minutes, until the broccoli is cooked and slightly crisp. Serve hot with cucumber slices, if you like.

per serving
**carbs: 1.7 g  protein: 10 g  calories: 116  fiber: 2 g  fat: 9 g (saturated fat: 1 g)**

# spanish tortilla with zucchini and manchego

**Choose a smallish, reliable non-stick pan for the tortilla, ideally about 10 inches in diameter. This may seem too small for the initial frying of the zucchini, but it does work, creating the perfect, juicy thickness.**

1 lb 10 oz/750 g zucchini, thinly sliced

2 tbsp olive oil

3 organic eggs

3½ oz/100 g Manchego or other hard cheese, cut into small dice

sea salt and freshly ground black pepper

Serves 6

Heat a small, non-stick skillet over a medium, heat and add 1 tbsp olive oil. Add the zucchini, season with a little salt and pepper and cook, moving them around frequently, until soft and golden.

Break the eggs into a large bowl and beat well with a little salt and pepper. Stir the zucchini and cheese into the eggs until the zucchini are well coated.

Return the pan to the heat and add the remaining olive oil. Scoop the egg mixture into the pan.

Cook, loosening the edges occasionally, until the tortilla is deep golden underneath and loose when you shake the pan. Slide on to a plate, place another plate on top and carefully flip over. Slide the tortilla back into the pan and cook until the other side is golden and the egg is cooked throughout. Remove from the pan and cool. Serve warm or cold, cut into wedges.

**per serving**
**carbs: 2.5 g  protein: 10 g  calories: 187  fiber: 1 g  fat: 15 g (saturated fat: 5 g)**

# 04: main courses

Feed your friends and family with these substantial dishes—tarts, gratins, stews, curries and comfort food. Even those not on a low-carb diet can't fail to feel satisfied.

# vietnamese asparagus pancakes

**This coconut batter is something that I dreamed up, but it fits deliciously into a Vietnamese-style pancake platter, with the essential cucumber and herb salad and hot-sweet sauce. If asparagus is out of season, try using lightly stir-fried beansprouts instead.**

2 bunches asparagus,
about 9 oz/250 g total
4 tsp sunflower oil
4 green onions, sliced

**For the batter**
4 tbsp soy flour
3 organic eggs
½ cup/3½ fl oz/100 ml
canned coconut milk
½ tsp ground turmeric
large pinch of salt

**To serve**
½ cucumber, about
5 oz/150 g, sliced
4 cilantro sprigs
4 fresh mint sprigs
1 recipe Sweet Chili
Sauce (see *page 132*)

Serves 4

Preheat the oven to 250°F/120°C for keeping warm. Steam the asparagus in a pan or in the microwave for 3 minutes, or until cooked to your liking. Keep warm.

To make the batter, place the flour, eggs, coconut milk, turmeric, and salt in a blender and process until smooth. Heat a medium, non-stick skillet over a medium heat and add 1 tsp oil. Pour in a quarter of the batter in a thin layer and swirl the pan to coat the base. Sprinkle with a quarter of the green onions before it sets. When golden underneath, flip the pancake over and cook until golden on the other side. Transfer to a plate and keep warm. Make three more pancakes in the same way, adding 1 tsp oil to the pan each time.

To serve, roll a pancake around a bundle of asparagus, starting from the edge. Serve with cucumber, cilantro, and mint sprigs, and a small bowl of sweet chili sauce.

per serving
carbs: 7 g  protein: 14 g  calories: 230  fiber: 3.6 g  fat: 16 g (saturated fat: 2 g)

Illustrated on *page 70*.

# arugula and ricotta cheesecake

A creamy, savory cheesecake, lightened with arugula and herbs. Serve with an arugula salad, or for a more "full-on" meal, with Braised Fennel and Bell Peppers (see *page 106*).

**butter, for greasing**
**¾ cup/3 oz/75 g walnut**
**  pieces**
**1 tbsp olive oil**
**3 garlic cloves, chopped**
**3 green onions, chopped**
**7 oz/200 g arugula,**
**  coarsely chopped**
**3 tbsp chopped fresh herbs,**
**  such as parsley, basil**
**  and dill**
**3 organic eggs**
**2½ cups/1¼ lb/500 g ricotta**
**  cheese, drained**
**4 tbsp freshly grated**
**  Parmesan cheese**
**sea salt and freshly ground**
**  black pepper**

Serves 6

Preheat the oven to 325°F/160°C. Generously butter a 8 inch cake pan with a loose base. Grind the walnut pieces to a powder in a food processor, then press them into the base and sides of the pan.

Heat a skillet over a low heat and add the olive oil. Cook the garlic and green onions for 1 minute, until fragrant. Add the arugula and herbs and stir for 1–2 minutes, until the arugula is just wilted. Remove the pan from the heat.

Put the eggs, ricotta, Parmesan, and the arugula mixture in a clean food processor and season with salt and pepper. Process until evenly mixed. Pour into the prepared pan. Bake for about 45 minutes, until golden and firm. Serve warm.

per serving
**carbs: 3 g  protein: 15 g  calories: 293  fiber: 0.8 g  fat: 24 g (saturated fat: 9 g)**

# warm salad of eggplant and melting camembert

**Get ready for some guilt-free indulgence with this upmarket salad. Salting the eggplants will prevent them from absorbing too much oil.**

2 medium eggplants, sliced
  into ½ inch rounds
olive oil
4 shallots, sliced
½ cup/3½ fl oz/100 ml
  dry vermouth or
  white wine
1 tbsp wine vinegar
2 radicchio or treviso,
  leaves torn
1 cup/4½ oz/125 g young
  spinach leaves
7 oz/200 g chilled
  Camembert cheese,
  sliced into strips
½ cup/2 oz/50g walnuts,
  lightly crushed
handful of fresh mint
  leaves, chopped
salt and freshly ground
  black pepper

Serves 4

Spread out the eggplant rounds in a colander and sprinkle with salt. Leave to drain for 30 minutes, then pat dry.

Heat a large skillet over a medium heat and add 4 tbsp olive oil. Cook the eggplants, in batches if necessary, until soft and golden, adding a little more oil if necessary. Remove the eggplants and add a drop more oil to the pan, then cook the shallots until soft. Return all the eggplants to the pan and reheat.

Add the vermouth or wine all at once—stand back as it may splutter at first. Season well with salt and pepper and cook, shaking the pan gently, until the liquid has reduced by half. Add the vinegar to the pan and shake. Cook for a further 2 minutes, while the juices thicken and caramelize, then remove the pan from the heat. Preheat the broiler to its highest setting.

Meanwhile, make a bed of radicchio and young spinach leaves on a heatproof platter. Top with eggplants and pan juices. Place slices of Camembert on the summit. Sprinkle with walnuts. Place the platter under the broiler until the cheese starts to melt. Finally, sprinkle with chopped mint and serve.

**per serving**
**carbs: 5 g  protein: 1 g  calories: 162  fiber: 2 g  fat: 13 g (saturated fat: 2 g)**

Illustrated on front cover.

# creamy celery root gratin

This makes a generous quantity, and believe me, you are going to want leftovers! It also freezes well. Serve with Swiss Chard with Pine Nuts and Redcurrants (see *page 107*).

butter, for greasing
3 garlic cloves
1 tsp coarse salt
1 large celery root,
    1½ lb/700 g trimmed
    weight, peeled and grated
generous grinding of
    nutmeg
1¼ cups/½ pint/300 ml
    heavy or whipping cream
½ cup/2 oz/50 g ground
    almonds
2 tbsp chopped fresh
    parsley
4 tbsp freshly grated
    Parmesan cheese
salt and freshly ground
    black pepper

Serves 8

Preheat oven to 400°F/200°C. Lightly grease a gratin dish.

Crush the garlic in a mortar with the salt until smooth (alternatively use a garlic crusher).

Mix together the salted garlic, celery root, nutmeg, and cream in a large bowl and season with pepper. Stir until well mixed—it helps to use clean hands to combine the mixture thoroughly. Spoon the mixture into the gratin dish and pack down.

Mix together the almonds, parsley, and Parmesan. Sprinkle over the top of the gratin. Bake for about 40 minutes, until soft and golden.

per serving
carbs: 3 g  protein: 6 g  calories: 271  fiber: 4 g  fat: 26 g (saturated fat: 14 g)

# spaghetti squash
# with smoked chili pesto

**Some purists might say "Don't mess with pesto," but trust me, this combination works (see also Smoky Eggplant Timbales, *page 34*). The noodle-like squash, with its low-key flavor, is a perfect partner for this assertive pesto.**

olive oil
**1 large spaghetti squash,
    about 1 lb 10 oz/750 g**
⅓ **cup/1 oz/25 g freshly
    grated Parmesan cheese
    (optional)**

**For the smoked
    chili pesto**
**1 dried smoked chili, such
    as chipotle (optional)**
**2 tsp smoked paprika**
**large bunch of basil**
½ **cup/3½ oz/100 g
    pine nuts**
**2 garlic cloves**
⅔ **cup/2 oz/50 g freshly
    grated Parmesan cheese**
½ **tsp sea salt, or to taste**
**6 tbsp olive oil**

Serves 4

Preheat the oven to 400°F/200°C. Lightly oil a cookie sheet. Cut the spaghetti squash in half from stem to base and scoop out the seeds and surrounding fibers. Place cut side down on the cookie sheet and cook for 45–60 minutes, or until a skewer or fork pushed through the skin meets no resistance underneath. Leave until cool enough to handle. Leave the oven turned on.

Meanwhile, make the pesto. If using the dried chili, place it in a small pan with boiling water and simmer for 15–20 minutes, until soft and rehydrated. Cool, de-seed and chop. Place the remaining pesto ingredients, except the olive oil, in a food processor with the chopped chili and process until finely chopped. With the motor running, gradually add the oil until a thick paste forms.

Use a fork to pull all the spaghetti-like strands of squash away from the skin. Place in a bowl and toss with the pesto—if it seems difficult to distribute, a little splash of boiling water will help. Spoon into an ovenproof dish, sprinkle with the Parmesan, if using, and bake for 10–15 minutes, until heated through. Alternatively, simply reheat in a microwave until piping hot throughout.

**per serving
carbs: 10 g  protein: 13 g  calories: 462  fiber: 5 g  fat: 41 g (saturated fat: 8 g)**

# thai hot and sour salad
# with crispy tofu

Here's a user-friendly version of the classic Thai salad *"som tum."* Low-carb rutabaga takes the place of green papaya and the tofu bumps up the protein quotient.

7 oz/200 g firm tofu
peanut oil or
   sunflower oil, for frying

**For the dressing**
2 red chilis, de-seeded
   if large
2 garlic cloves
4 tbsp light soy sauce
4 tbsp lime juice
4 tbsp sweetener

**For the salad**
11 oz/300 g rutabaga,
   grated
⅔ cup/3½ oz/100 g green
   beans, sliced lengthways
1 red bell pepper, cored
   and thinly sliced
4 green onions, sliced
2 handfuls of fresh
   mint leaves
½ cup/2 oz/50 g toasted
   peanuts, ground

Serves 4

First, drain the tofu and wrap in paper towels until ready to use.

Make the dressing by pounding all the ingredients in a heavy mortar or by processing them in a blender. Combine the rutabaga, beans, bell pepper, green onions, mint, and half the peanuts. Stir half the dressing through the salad.

Heat a shallow layer of oil in a skillet over a high heat. Cut the tofu into 3 inch slices and fry, turning once, until golden all over. Drain on paper towels.

Spoon the salad on to plates and top with the tofu. Finish with the remaining dressing and sprinkle with the remaining peanuts.

per serving
**carbs: 10 g  protein: 10 g  calories: 159  fiber: 3.5 g  fat: 9 g (saturated fat: 1.5 g)**

Illustrated on *page 72*.

# tomato and artichoke stew

**Canned or bottled artichoke hearts are a great convenience food and make this a sumptuous yet user-friendly dish. I originally made this dish using four large fresh artichoke hearts. Do try it with fresh if you're feeling up to the rather hairy process of removing all the leaves and the choke, then simmer in the sauce until tender.**

3 tbsp olive oil

4 garlic cloves, crushed with
   1 tsp coarse salt in a
   mortar or with a
   garlic crusher

2 x 14 oz/400 g cans
   tomatoes, chopped

11 oz/300 g canned or
   bottled artichoke hearts,
   drained and halved
   if whole

1 tbsp red wine vinegar

2 tbsp chopped fresh flat
   leaf parsley

pinch of dried chili flakes

4 organic eggs

4–5 tbsp ricotta cheese

sea salt and freshly ground
   black pepper

Serves 4

Heat the oil in a large pan. Add the garlic and cook, stirring. As soon as it becomes fragrant, add the tomatoes and artichokes. Bring to the boil, then add the vinegar, parsley, and chili. Season to taste with salt, if necessary, and pepper. Cover and simmer gently, stirring occasionally, for 10 minutes, then remove the lid and simmer for a further 10 minutes, until thickened.

Make four hollows with a spoon around the edge of the pan and break the eggs into them. Spoon ricotta in between the eggs. Cover the pan while the eggs cook. As soon as they are poached to your liking, serve the stew.

per serving
carbs: 8 g  protein: 13 g  calories: 233  fiber: 1.5 g  fat: 17 g (saturated fat: 4 g)

# paneer masala
# with spinach and coconut

**I've borrowed techniques from various regions of India's vast and varied cuisine for this quick stir-fry dish. The result may not be authentic, but it is certainly an exciting combination, and amazingly simple to prepare. Use store-bought paneer or discover how easy it is to make from scratch on *page 129*.**

2 tbsp sunflower oil
1 tsp black mustard seeds
1 tsp cumin seeds
1 tsp ground turmeric
2 red chilis, slit
3 green onions, sliced
3 garlic cloves, sliced
1 inch piece of fresh
   ginger, chopped
⅔ cup/2 oz/50 g dry
   shredded unsweetened
   coconut
11 oz/300 g paneer, diced
7 oz/200 g young spinach,
   chopped
½ cup/3½ fl oz/100 ml
   Greek (strained plain)
   yogurt

Serves 4

Heat a wok until moderately hot. Add the oil and mustard seeds. When the seeds pop, add the cumin, turmeric, chilis, green onions, garlic, and ginger and cook for about 2 minutes, until golden and fragrant. Add the coconut and paneer and cook until the paneer becomes light golden in color.

Stir the spinach through the mixture and as soon as it is completely wilted, remove the wok from the heat. Stir in the yogurt and serve hot.

per serving
carbs: 5 g  protein: 12 g  calories: 236  fiber: 3 g  fat: 18 g (saturated fat: 10 g)

# tunisian spiced torte

This delicious crustless quiche is inspired by a recipe from Tunisia called *"Makhouda nahna."* I first came across it in *North Africa—The Vegetarian Table* by Kitty Morse, a wonderful book now sadly out of print. The torte keeps for days in the refrigerator and is extremely portable, making it perfect for a picnic.

butter, for greasing
2 tbsp olive oil
2 onions, chopped
10 organic eggs
1 cup/3½ oz/100 g
    ground almonds
generous handful of fresh
    parsley, chopped
1½ tbsp dried mint
1 tbsp smoked paprika
9 oz/250 g Gruyère cheese,
    diced
½ tsp salt
freshly ground black pepper

Serves 8

Preheat the oven to 400°F/200°C. Generously grease a 9 inch springform cake pan.

Heat the olive oil over a medium heat and cook the onions until lightly browned.

Beat the eggs in a large bowl, then stir in all remaining ingredients and add the onions. Stir until thoroughly mixed. Pour mixture into the prepared pan and bake for 45–50 minutes, until a knife inserted in the middle comes out clean.

Leave to cool slightly, then run a sharp knife around the edge, unmold and serve warm or at room temperature.

per serving
carbs: 3 g  protein: 21 g  calories: 345  fiber: 1 g  fat: 28 g (saturated fat: 10 g)

# spinach and ricotta gnocchi with sage butter

**These rich, yet fluffy gnocchi are a proper Italian luxury meal. They can also be placed in an ovenproof dish after boiling, covered in grated Gruyère and baked for a fabulous gratin.**

1⅓ cups/7 oz/200 g young
   spinach, washed
2 tbsp chopped parsley
1 garlic clove, crushed
⅔ cup/5 oz/150 g ricotta
   cheese, drained
⅔ cup/3 oz/75g soy flour
1 organic egg, plus 1 yolk
1 cup/3½ oz/100 g freshly
   grated Parmesan cheese,
   plus extra to serve
generous grating of nutmeg
salt and freshly ground
   black pepper

**For the sage butter**
6 tbsp/3 oz/75 g unsalted
   butter
pinch of salt
16 fresh sage leaves,
   coarsely chopped

Serves 4

Place the spinach in a bowl and pour boiling water over it. When it has wilted, drain and leave to cool. Wrap a clean dish cloth around the spinach and, holding it over the sink, squeeze out as much moisture as possible. Chop finely.

Combine the chopped spinach with the parsley, garlic, ricotta, soy flour, egg and egg yolk, Parmesan, and nutmeg. Season with salt and pepper. Stir vigorously until thoroughly combined.

Bring a large pan of water to the boil and salt it well. Form the dough into balls, about two-thirds the size of a golf ball. (The gnocchi can be frozen at this stage if you're planning a future meal.) Drop a few gnocchi at a time into the water, lower the heat to a simmer and cook for 3–4 minutes, until they have risen to the surface. Remove with a slotted spoon. Keep warm while you cook the remaining gnocchi.

To make the sage butter, melt the butter in a pan over a medium heat. Add a pinch of salt and the sage. Cook until the sage is tinged with gold. Pour the herb butter over the cooked gnocchi and serve.

per serving
**carbs: 6 g  protein: 22 g  calories: 409  fiber: 3 g  fat: 33 g (saturated fat: 18 g)**

Illustrated on *page 74*.

# egg foo yung

I consulted Norman Fu, Chef Lecturer in Chinese Cookery, to find out the secret of this classic Anglo-Chinese dish. It requires a smart trick (outlined below) to cook it to perfection—not too leaky and not too solid. Also, the eggs are cooked over a medium-low heat, because as Norman insists, "A good *foo yung* does not have any brown bits." No spices or sauces are used, because they just mask the delicate flavors of the dish.

2½ tbsp peanut oil or
   sunflower oil
3 tbsp chopped red bell
   pepper
3 tbsp chopped celery
3 tbsp chopped zucchini
¼ cup/1 oz/25 g
   beansprouts
3 green onions, sliced
4 organic eggs
sea salt

Serves 2

Line a small colander with paper towels. Heat a well-seasoned wok or non-stick skillet over a high heat and add 1 tsp of the oil. Add the bell pepper, celery, zucchini, beansprouts, green onions, and a pinch of salt and stir-fry for 1–2 minutes, until softened. Transfer the contents of the pan to the lined colander and leave to cool and drain. This makes sure that the egg will not be diluted with cooking juices.

Beat the eggs with a little salt until mixed but not frothy. Stir in the cooled vegetables and mix well. Heat the wok or pan over a low to medium heat and add the remaining oil. Pour in the egg mixture and swirl in the pan. Push the mixture away from you while tilting the pan towards you, rather than scrambling vigorously, so the mixture runs gently on to the exposed areas. Repeat this action all over the pan until the egg is just set. Turn the whole *foo yung* over once, then slide on to a plate and serve immediately.

per serving
carbs: 3.5 g  protein: 16 g  calories: 293  fiber: 1 g  fat: 25 g (saturated fat: 5 g)

Main Courses continue on *page 77*.

almond muffins (*page 27*) and melon berry power smoothie (*page 19*)

red bell pepper and goat's cheese timbale (*page 35*)

curried celery root soup with cilantro oil (*page 43*) with sesame and black pepper crispbreads (*page 89*)

tofu, mint and palm heart salad with hot and spicy dressing (*page 45*) and fragrant coconut broth (*page 32*)

cyprus salad (*page 49*)

vietnamese asparagus pancakes (*page 54*) with sweet chili sauce (*page 132*)

artichoke stuffed with creamy wild mushrooms (*page 83*)

thai hot and sour salad with crispy tofu (*page 59*)

provençal tian (*page 78*)

spinach and ricotta gnocchi with sage butter (*page 63*)

green bean and roasted bell pepper parcels (*page 101*) and eggplant and smoked cheese involtini (*page 95*)

rose and raspberry pudding (*page 122*) and lemon custard macaroon tart (*page 118*)

# luxury cauliflower cheese

**Here's my variation on the classic comfort food, best served with a very simply dressed salad of crunchy leaves.**

2 large trimmed leeks, about 11 oz/300 g

1 large cauliflower, about 1¼ lb/500 g, broken into florets

1 tsp sea salt

2 bay leaves

1¼ cups/½ pint/300 ml water

1 cup/7 oz/200 g cream cheese

1 cup/3½ oz/100 g grated Gruyère cheese

4 tbsp freshly grated Parmesan cheese

½ tsp dried chili flakes, or to taste

Serves 4

Preheat the oven to 425°F/220°C. Slice the leeks quite thickly and wash well, making sure no dirt is concealed in the upper parts. Place the leeks in a large pan. Place the cauliflower florets on top. Add the salt and bay leaves and pour in the water. Cover and bring to the boil over a high heat. Lower the heat and simmer for 5 minutes.

Remove the cauliflower, leeks and bay leaves from the pan and reserve the cooking liquid. Place the vegetables in a wide roasting pan or gratin dish in a snug single layer. Put the dish of vegetables in the oven to dry out while you prepare the cheese sauce.

Bring the reserved cooking liquid to the boil. Add the cream cheese, breaking it up with a whisk. Whisk until smooth and melted. Add the grated Gruyère and whisk until melted and thick, then remove from the heat.

Remove the vegetables from the oven and pour the cheese sauce evenly over them. Sprinkle the grated Parmesan over the top and dust with chili flakes. Return to the oven and bake for about 30 minutes, until golden brown and bubbly.

**per serving**
**carbs: 6 g  protein: 18 g  calories: 422  fiber: 4 g  fat: 36 g (saturated fat: 22 g)**

# provençal tian

**The arrangement of the vegetables in three colorful stripes makes this a *piece de resistance*, although you can just throw it all in haphazardly without affecting the flavor. The recipe makes a generous quantity—leftovers are lovely to eat cold as a salad.**

butter, for greasing
1 red bell pepper, cored
   and sliced into rings
1½ cups/12 oz/350 g vine or
   plum tomatoes, sliced
1½ cups/12 oz/350 g zucchini,
   sliced in ½ inch rounds
14 oz/400 g artichoke hearts,
   drained and halved
1½ cups/12 oz/350 g
   eggplant, sliced in
   ¼ inch rounds
1⅓ cups/11 oz/300 g fennel,
   sliced
½ cup/2 oz/50 g good-
   quality black olives
4 bay leaves
7 oz/200 g fresh goat's
   cheese (optional)
freshly ground black pepper

For the dressing
4 tbsp olive oil
1 tbsp balsamic vinegar
4 garlic cloves, thinly sliced
a handful of fresh basil,
   shredded
2 tbsp capers
1 tsp salt, or to taste

Serves 8

Preheat the oven to 400°F/200°C. Lightly grease a wide rectangular ovenproof dish. Aim to alternate each pair of vegetables with one another: place the red bell pepper and tomatoes alternately in one red stripe across the top of the dish, and the zucchini and artichoke hearts in one green stripe across the bottom. Arrange the slices of eggplant and fennel in the middle.

Whisk together all the dressing ingredients and spoon almost all the mixture over the vegetables as evenly as possible. Brush every exposed surface with the remaining dressing. Season with plenty of pepper and garnish with olives and bay leaves.

Roast for 45–50 minutes, until the vegetables are soft, sizzling and well-browned around the edges. Remove from the oven and crumble the goat's cheese, if using, over the surface. Serve warm or cold.

per serving
**carbs: 6 g  protein: 9 g  calories: 180  fiber: 3 g  fat: 13 g (saturated fat: 6 g)**

Illustrated on *page 73*.

# cauliflower mash and porcini gravy for sausages

The vegetarian sausages available nowadays get better and better as food technology improves. Many are soy-protein based and low-carb, but do check the label. There's a small amount of wheat flour in this gravy—soy flour simply doesn't do the same job—but it's only a little.

**For the mash**
1 lb 5 oz/600 g large
    cauliflower,
    trimmed weight
½ tsp salt
1 tbsp olive oil
generous grinding of
    nutmeg

**For the gravy**
⅛ cup/¼ oz/10g dried
    porcini mushrooms
1 cup/8 fl oz/250 ml boiling
    water
2 tbsp olive oil
1 leek, chopped
1 tbsp all-purpose flour
leaves stripped from 2 fresh
    thyme sprigs
1 bay leaf
½ cup/4 fl oz/12 ml dry
    vermouth or white wine
sea salt and freshly ground
    black pepper

vegetarian sausages

Serves 4

First, make the gravy. Place the porcini mushrooms in a bowl and pour the boiling water over them. Leave to soak for about 20 minutes, then drain, reserving the soaking liquid, and chop the mushrooms.

Heat a skillet over a medium heat and add the oil. Add the chopped leek and porcini and cook for about 3 minutes, until the leek is softened. Add the flour and cook for 1 minute, then add the herbs, vermouth or wine, and the reserved soaking water, and season with salt and pepper. Bring to the boil and cook until slightly thickened.

To make the mash, chop the cauliflower into fairly small pieces. Place in a heavy pan with the salt and oil and stir. Cover and place over a medium heat until steaming, then lower the heat to a gentle simmer. Let the cauliflower cook in its own juice for 15–20 minutes, until very soft and collapsed. Remove the lid and let any remaining juices evaporate. Grind or grate in a generous flavoring of nutmeg, then mash until smooth. If it still seems too wet, continue steaming over the heat, stirring frequently.

Cook the vegetarian sausages according to the manufacturer's instructions. Serve the mash with the sausages and porcini gravy poured over the top.

per serving
carbs: 10 g  protein: 7 g  calories: 174  fiber: 3.5 g  fat: 10 g (saturated fat: 1.5 g)

# paneer and herb fritters

**A few of these delectable, crunchy little cakes make a satisfying meal with salad or green vegetables. Alternatively, make tiny fritters for party nibbles. You can use store-bought paneer, or make your own using the recipe on *page 129*.**

9 oz/250 g paneer, grated
   or crumbled
1 cup/2 oz/50 g cilantro
   sprigs and mint leaves,
   chopped
1 inch piece of fresh
   ginger, finely grated
2 garlic cloves, crushed
1 tsp coriander seeds,
   crushed, or
   1 tsp ground coriander
1 tsp salt
2 organic eggs
2 tbsp soy flour
peanut oil or
   sunflower oil, for frying
freshly ground black pepper
lemon wedges, to serve

Serves 4

Combine the paneer, herbs, ginger, garlic, coriander seeds, salt, eggs, and flour in a bowl, season with pepper and mix very thoroughly. Using wet hands, take walnut-sized handfuls of the mixture, then squeeze and press into little flat patties. Set aside on a plate while you make all the cakes. Chill in the refrigerator until ready to cook.

Heat a shallow layer of oil in a non-stick pan over a medium heat. When hot, add the patties to the oil and cook until golden, then turn over and cook until golden all over. Drain on kitchen paper. Serve with lemon wedges to squeeze over them.

per serving
carbs: 4 g  protein: 14 g  calories: 165  fiber: 1 g  fat: 10 g (saturated fat: 3 g)

# pumpkin curry

This delicious southern Indian style curry can be eaten on its own as a stew or ladled over a thick bed of lightly buttered leaf spinach (cooked from fresh or frozen). Use ordinary, "jack-o-lantern" type pumpkin for the lightest carb ratio. Although orange-fleshed squashes, such as butternut and acorn, will work beautifully, they do have a slightly higher carbohydrate count.

**For the spice paste**
3 garlic cloves
1 inch piece of fresh
   ginger, grated
1 tsp coriander seeds
1 tsp cumin seeds
½ tsp ground turmeric
1 tsp chili flakes
½ tsp sea salt

2 tbsp peanut oil or
   sunflower oil
1 cup/7 oz/200 g pumpkin,
   peeled, de-seeded and cut
   into chunks
1 cup/7 oz/200 g zucchini,
   cut into chunks
⅔ cup/4 oz/125 g celery,
   sliced
14 oz/400 g can coconut milk
1 cup/7 oz/200 g canned
   chopped tomatoes
4 organic eggs
sea salt and freshly ground
   black pepper
chopped cilantro, to garnish
   (optional)

Serves 4

First, make the spice paste. Place all ingredients in a blender or spice grinder. Add enough water to allow the blades to run smoothly and process until a smooth, pourable paste results.

Heat a wok or large pan over a medium heat. Add the oil and when it's hot, add the pumpkin, zucchini, and celery and stir-fry for about 2 minutes, until starting to soften. Pour in the spice paste and stir briskly for 1–2 minutes, until fragrant and evenly distributed. Add the coconut milk and tomatoes and season well with salt and pepper. Bring to the boil, then lower the heat to a simmer. Cook, stirring frequently, for about 30 minutes, until the pumpkin has softened so much that it begins to melt into the thick curry sauce.

Meanwhile, cook the eggs. Place them in a small pan and cover with cold water. Bring to the boil and cook for 5 minutes, then drain and cool under cold running water. Shell and slice in half.

When the curry is cooked, stir well, then lay the egg halves on the surface of the curry. Simmer for 2 minutes, without stirring, until the eggs are warmed through. Sprinkle coriander leaves over the curry and serve.

**per serving**
**carbs: 8 g  protein: 12 g  calories: 344  fiber: 1.5 g  fat: 30 g (saturated fat: 3 g)**

# cabbage gratin

**Here, the modest cabbage gets dressed to the nines in a creamy golden crust, studded with caraway and lifted with the flavor of orange rind. Serve with steamed green beans.**

1 tbsp olive oil
3 garlic cloves, chopped
1 lb 5 oz/600 g large Savoy
   cabbage, trimmed weight,
   shredded
1¾ cups/14 fl oz/400 ml
   reduced-fat sour cream
3 organic egg yolks
¼ cup/2 oz/50 g grated
   Cheddar cheese
finely grated rind of 1 orange
several fresh thyme sprigs,
   leaves stripped
1 tsp caraway seeds
salt and freshly ground
   black pepper

Serves 4

Heat the oil in a pan and cook the garlic until light golden. Add the cabbage and season well. Cover and cook, stirring frequently, for about 15 minutes, until the cabbage is tender.

Preheat the oven to 400°F/200°C. Remove the pan from the heat. If there is liquid in the pan, drain it off. Spoon the cabbage into an ovenproof dish and pack down.

To make the custard, beat together the sour cream, egg yolks, Cheddar, orange rind, and thyme leaves with a pinch of salt. Pour the mixture over the cabbage and sprinkle with the caraway seeds. Bake for 30–40 minutes, until the top is golden and bubbling around the edges.

per serving
**carbs: 10 g  protein: 10 g  calories: 323  fiber: 3.5 g  fat: 26 g (saturated fat: 14 g)**

# artichokes stuffed with creamy wild mushrooms

**You might call this "gilding the lily"—it's hard to improve on the perfect globe artichoke, boiled whole and served with melted butter or mayonnaise. This recipe does elevate it, however, not only to red-carpet status, but renders it a complete meal with minimum effort. Enjoy.**

2 tbsp white wine vinegar

2 tbsp olive oil

1 tbsp/½ oz/15 g butter

4 large fresh globe artichokes

4½ cups11 oz/300 g mixed wild mushrooms, especially morels, chanterelles and ceps, chopped into small chunks

2 tsp fresh thyme or lemon thyme leaves

5 tbsp dry vermouth

⅔ cup/5 oz/150 g mascarpone cheese

½ cup/2 oz/50 g walnuts, crushed

a handful of flat leaf parsley leaves, chopped

salt and freshly ground black pepper

*Serves 4*

Bring a large pan of water to the boil. Add the vinegar, olive oil, and plenty of salt to the water.

Meanwhile, prepare the artichokes. Snap off the stems and slice about one-third off the top. Pull out what you can from the middle and use a spoon to scoop out all of the hairy choke. Place in the boiling water and cook for 30–40 minutes, until tender. They are done when a leaf pulled from near the center comes away without resistance. Drain upside down until dry. Preheat the oven to 425°F/220°C.

To make the stuffing, melt the butter in a wide skillet over a medium heat and add the mushrooms and thyme with a sprinkling of salt and pepper. When they have absorbed the butter and begin to soften, pour in the vermouth and cook, stirring, until it has almost all evaporated. Finally, stir in the mascarpone. Stir until the mushrooms are evenly coated.

Spoon the mixture into the middle of the drained artichokes. Sprinkle with crushed walnuts and bake for 10–15 minutes, until heated through and golden on top. Garnish with chopped parsley before serving. When eating, use the leaves of the artichoke to scoop out the creamy filling.

**per serving**
**carbs: 3.5 g  protein: 6.5 g  calories: 324  fiber: 1 g  fat: 30 g (saturated fat: 14 g)**

Illustrated on *page 71*.

# 05: nibbles, snacks and quick fixes

It used to be so easy to reach for a sandwich or a bag of chips—low-carb life is different. A mouthful of impact-flavored protein or tasty, vitamin-packed veggies are the solution, and it's still easy.

# chili-crust brazil nuts

**Roasting brings out the best flavor in nuts, and these have an added flavor dimension. When roasting nuts, it's essential to use a timer, as the short cooking time means they so easily get forgotten.**

**1 tbsp olive oil**
**2 tsp dark soy sauce**
**1 tsp lemon juice**
**1 tsp sweetener**
**1 tsp paprika**
**½ tsp crushed chili flakes**
**1 tsp sesame seeds**
**1¼ cups/5 oz/150 g Brazil nuts**

Serves 8

Preheat oven to 375°F/190°C. Whisk together all the ingredients except the Brazil nuts. Stir in the nuts and coat evenly. Spread them out in a single layer on a cookie sheet and roast, stirring every 2 minutes, until golden.

Cool completely, then transfer to a bowl and serve. Store in an airtight container.

**per serving**
**carbs: 0.6 g  protein: 2.6 g  calories: 141  fiber: 0.8 g  fat: 14 g (saturated fat: 3.2 g)**

# celery with pesto

**Here's an easy solution when you're in the mood to raid the refrigerator. You can use ready-made pesto or make your own (see *page 131*).**

**2 celery sticks, trimmed**
**2 tbsp cream cheese**
**1 tsp pesto**
**freshly ground black pepper**

Serves 2

Use a butter knife to spread the cream cheese inside the curve of the celery. Drizzle pesto down the middle. Grind over some pepper, then eat whole or slice diagonally into bite-size pieces.

**per serving**
**carbs: 0.4 g  protein: 0.6 g  calories: 70  fiber: 0.3 g  fat: 7 g (saturated fat: 4 g)**

# edam crisps

This method can be applied to some other hard cheeses, including Gouda, but in my experience, Edam gets the best results every time. A reliable non-stick pan is the only tool for the job. Pre-sliced cheese is recommended, as it may be more thinly sliced than you can manage yourself.

3½ oz/100 g Edam cheese,
  sliced into 8 very
  thin pieces

Makes 8

Lay the cheese slices in a non-stick pan, leaving a space of at least ½ inch between them. You may have to cook in batches if your pan is too small. Place the pan over the lowest possible heat.

The cheese will bubble and pop, oil will ooze out and eventually the cheese will start to turn crisp underneath. Cook until the underside is looking dry and very slightly golden. This may take up to 15 minutes. Turn the cheese over carefully and cook the other side for about 5 minutes until crisp. Drain the cheese crisps on paper towels. Serve warm or cold.

per serving
carbs: 0 g  protein: 3 g  calories: 43  fiber: 0 g  fat: 3 g (saturated fat: 2 g)

# parmesan wafers

These feather-light savory wafers are best enjoyed straight out of the oven or soon afterwards. They soften slightly as they cool, but can be re-crisped in the oven later (4–5 minutes at 350°F/180°C).

2 organic egg whites
pinch of cream of tartar
3 tbsp finely grated
  Parmesan cheese

Makes 8

Preheat the oven to 300°F/150°C. Beat the egg whites with the cream of tartar in a grease-free bowl until stiff but not dry. Gently fold in the Parmesan, keeping the mixture light and airy, until evenly incorporated. Spoon on to a parchment-lined cookie sheet to make eight wafers and bake for about 15 minutes, until golden and crisp.

per serving
carbs: 0 g  protein: 1.5 g  calories: 13  fiber: 0 g  fat: 0.7 g (saturated fat: 0.5 g)

# mexican cucumbers

I was first introduced to these in Mexico, where they are served as bar snacks—it's a surprisingly good combination. The mild chili powder I use is a commonly sold mixture with added garlic powder and oregano.

1 medium cucumber, about
   11 oz/300 g
2 limes
2 tsp mild chili powder
sea salt

Serves 8

Trim the ends of the cucumber, then cut it across into four pieces of equal length. Cut each piece lengthways into eight wedges. Arrange the wedges skin side down in a dish and squeeze the juice from the limes over them. Sprinkle with an even coat of mild chili powder and season with salt.

per serving
carbs: 0.5 g  protein: 0.3 g  calories: 4  fiber: 0.3 g  fat: 0 g (saturated fat: 0 g)

# olive raisins

Virtually carbohydrate-free, olives are a great snack. This roasting technique gives them pleasingly chewy texture. Feel free to experiment with different spices—fennel seeds give a fragrant crunch.

1¾ cups/7 oz/200 g large
   pitted green olives
½ tsp fennel seeds
½ tsp chili flakes
2 tbsp olive oil

Serves 4

Preheat the oven to 400°F/200°C. Place the olives in a small ovenproof dish and stir in the remaining ingredients to coat evenly. Roast for 25–30 minutes, until shrunken and wrinkly. Leave to cool before serving.

per serving
carbs: 0 g  protein: 0.5 g  calories: 100  fiber: 1.5 g  fat: 11 g (saturated fat: 1.5 g)

# sesame and black pepper crispbreads

**When you really miss that cracker-crunch, these are a godsend. Cooking this batter in a microwave seems to be the only way to get a super-crisp result. They are a great companion to the soups in this book.**

**2 tbsp sesame seeds**
**olive oil, for brushing**
**½ cup/2 oz/50 g soy flour**
**1 organic egg**
**½ tsp salt**
**½ cup/4 fl oz/120 ml warm water**
**1 tsp freshly ground black pepper**

Makes 8

First toast the sesame seeds. Heat a dry skillet over a medium heat. Add the sesame seeds and toast, stirring frequently, until golden and popping. Remove from the pan and set aside.

Line a microwave-safe plate with non-stick baking parchment. Brush it generously with olive oil. Beat together the flour, egg, salt, water, and pepper until smooth. Pour a thin layer of batter on to the plate, about 2½ inches in diameter. Sprinkle with sesame seeds. Microwave on high for 2–3 minutes, until dry and crisp. Cool on a wire rack. Repeat with remaining batter.

**per serving**
**carbs: 1.5 g  protein: 4 g  calories: 65  fiber: 1 g  fat: 5 g (saturated fat: 0.8 g)**

Illustrated on *page 67*.

# spicy tofu jerky

**Deeply flavored and toothsome, these do a surprisingly good job of imitating beef jerky.**

7 oz/200 g smoked or
   plain firm tofu
2 tbsp dark soy sauce
2 tbsp dry sherry
1 tsp rice vinegar
pinch of cayenne pepper
1 tbsp sunflower oil

Makes 14

Preheat the oven to 250°F/120°C. Pat the tofu dry with paper towels, then slice very thinly into about 14 strips, about 1 inch wide, 3 inches long and roughly ⅛ inch thick.

Line a cookie sheet with non-stick baking parchment. Thoroughly whisk all the remaining ingredients together in a shallow dish. Dip each piece of tofu in the mixture, then lay on the cookie sheet. Spoon any remaining mixture carefully over the tofu strips.

Place in the oven and cook for about 60–80 minutes, until the tofu is crisp around the edges, but still pliable. Leave to cool. The strips can be stored in an airtight container in the refrigerator for up to 3 days.

**per serving**
**carbs: 0.3 g  protein: 1 g  calories: 21  fiber: 0 g  fat: 1.5 g (saturated fat: 0.2 g)**

# marinated crudité salad

**Here's a fantastic way of preparing raw vegetables which will keep in the refrigerator for a few days, ready to munch on any occasion.**

½ red bell pepper, cored
½ yellow bell pepper, cored
1⅓ cups/3½ oz/100 g sugar
  snap peas
⅔ cup/3½ oz/100 g fine
  green beans, trimmed
⅓ cup/2 oz/50 g zucchini
⅓ cup/2 oz/50 g celery
⅔ cup/3½ oz/100 g fennel
1 tbsp sea salt
1 tbsp extra virgin olive oil
1 tbsp lemon juice

Serves 4

If the vegetable lends itself to being cut into strips, do so; others can be cut into similar size pieces (for example, beans and fennel).

Place them all in a bowl and sprinkle with the salt. Toss with your hands to coat evenly. Transfer to a colander and leave over the sink, tossing occasionally, for 3–4 hours. When the juices have been drawn out and the vegetables are soft, return them to the rinsed-out bowl and drizzle with olive oil and lemon juice. Chill in the refrigerator until ready to eat.

per serving
**carbs: 5 g  protein: 2 g  calories: 57  fiber: 2.5 g  fat: 3 g (saturated fat: 0.5 g)**

# 06: party food

Canapes and finger food should be easy to make, easy to eat, beautiful, and luxurious. It's all possible with this chapter. Enjoy with champagne or vodka martinis.

# cucumber and tofu satay

On a day-to-day basis, I wouldn't normally fuss around threading bits on to skewers for supper, which is why this recipe lands in the Party Food chapter. However, I think you'll find these are easy and tasty enough to enjoy without a special occasion. Freezing the tofu gives it a remarkable fibrous texture which resembles chicken—try the technique below in other tofu dishes.

3½ oz/100 g firm tofu
3½ oz/100 g cucumber
1 recipe Satay Sauce (see *page 135*)

Makes 12

Freeze the tofu until completely solid, then thaw completely before using. Drain thoroughly and wrap in paper towels. Place on a plate and weigh down with a heavy object, such as a pan of water—this will compress the tofu slightly and squeeze out excess moisture. Leave for about 30 minutes, then cut into small cubes, about ½ inch wide.

Cut the cucumber into strips the same width and remove the seeds. Cut into pieces the same size as the tofu. Thread alternating pieces of tofu and cucumber on to 12 medium length bamboo skewers, using three of each per skewer. Lay the skewers side by side on a plate. Spoon satay sauce generously over them and serve.

per serving
carbs: 1 g  protein: 2 g  calories: 32  fiber: 0.5 g  fat: 2.5 g (saturated fat: 0.5 g)

# eggplant and smoked cheese involtini

**Involtini are simply "little rolls" in Italian. In this case, charbroiled eggplant slices encase little rod-shaped pieces of melting smoked cheese, which ideally should be a smoked mozzarella, but as it's rather a privilege to come across the real thing, any smoked cheese will do.**

2 eggplants,
    about 1 lb 5 oz/600 g,
    stem removed and sliced
    lengthways as thinly
    as possible
4 tbsp olive oil
3½ oz/100 g smoked
    mozzarella, smoked
    Cheddar or other smoked
    cheese, cut in 25 pieces,
    measuring about
    ¾ x ¼ inches
25 large fresh basil leaves
sea salt and freshly ground
    black pepper

Makes 25

Heat a grill pan for about 10 minutes, until very hot. Brush the eggplant slices lightly on both sides with olive oil. Cook on the grill pan until soft and striped with black on both sides. Season each slice with salt and pepper and leave to cool.

Place a basil leaf at one end of an eggplant slice and a piece of cheese on top of the basil. Roll the slice up around the cheese and basil. Place, seam side down, on a cookie sheet. Repeat with remaining ingredients.

Preheat the oven to 400°F/200°C. Just before serving, put the involtini in the oven for no longer than 5 minutes just to warm through—it's best to set a timer or they might overcook if forgotten. Serve warm and melting.

per serving
carbs: 0.5 g  protein: 1 g  calories: 30  fiber: 0.5 g  fat: 3 g (saturated fat: 1 g)

Illustrated on *page 75*.

# saffron aïoli with quail's eggs and asparagus

**Quail's eggs are wonderfully elegant, but undeniably awkward to peel. They are so beautiful in the shell, I always leave it on and let the guests do the work.**

24 quail's eggs
3 bunches asparagus, woody ends snapped off
3 organic egg yolks
5 garlic cloves
½ tsp saffron threads, soaked in 1 tbsp hot water, then ground in a mortar
salt
1 cup/8 fl oz/250 ml light olive oil
2 tbsp lemon juice

Serves 8

Place the quail's eggs in a pan and cover with cold water. Bring to the boil and cook for 3 minutes. Drain and cool under cold running water until completely cold.

Steam the asparagus until barely tender, or cooked to your liking. Cool.

Put the egg yolks, garlic, soaked saffron, soaking water, and a little salt in a food processor and process to combine. With the motor running, add the oil, one drop at a time. Gradually increase the pace and pour in the remaining oil in a very thin, steady stream until a thick mayonnaise is achieved. If the aïoli curdles, add another egg yolk.

Beat in the lemon juice. Scoop into a bowl and serve on a platter with quail's eggs and asparagus.

**per serving**
**carbs: 1.5 g  protein: 13 g  calories: 365  fiber: 1.3 g  fat: 34 g (saturated fat: 6 g)**

# tricolore skewers

**The three colors of the Italian flag, in one bite, on a skewer. Use buffalo milk mozzarella for the creamiest flavor; failing that, cow's milk, but always from a snow-white ball, not the "pizza cheese" type.**

**1 buffalo mozzarella, torn into 24 bite-size shreds**
**24 semi-dried, sunblush or sun-dried tomatoes in oil**
**24 large fresh basil leaves**

Makes 24

Pair up a piece of mozzarella and a tomato. Wrap a basil leaf around them and secure with a medium bamboo skewer. Serve immediately.

**per serving**
**carbs: 0.1 g  protein: 1.5 g  calories: 29  fiber: 0 g  fat: 2.5 g (saturated fat: 1 g)**

# cucumber with pink pickled ginger

**Pink pickled ginger is an essential accompaniment for sushi and can be found in Asian groceries and health food shops. Look out for the shredded psychedelic fuschia type (you can't miss it!), for maximum visual impact.**

**1 recipe Satay Sauce (see *page 135*)**
**half cucumber (about 5 inches, 7 oz/200 g)**
**4 tbsp/50 g pink pickled ginger**
**1 green onion, finely sliced diagonally**

Makes 20

Cool the Satay Sauce, then chill until thick.

Peel the cucumber and cut into 20 slices, ¼ inch thick. (If desired, you can make neat shapes with a small cookie cutter.)

Spoon a small dollop of Satay Sauce on each piece, then top with a pinch of pickled ginger. Garnish with a slice of green onion.

**per serving**
**carbs: 0.6 g  protein: 0.6 g  calories: 16  fiber: 0.2 g  fat: 1 g (saturated fat: 0.3 g)**

# chili citrus labneh platter

*"Labneh"* is a Middle Eastern soft fresh cheese made by transforming yogurt overnight in your refrigerator. It couldn't be simpler and you can flavor it with whatever you like—fresh or dried herbs, or whole toasted spices such as cumin. This red chili and citrus version is particularly pretty and the flavor just dances on the tongue.

2¼ cups/18 fl oz/500 ml
  Greek (strained plain)
  yogurt or other
  whole yogurt
2 red chilis, chopped
grated rind of 1 orange
grated rind of 1 lemon
extra virgin olive oil,
  for drizzling
salt

**to serve**
3 cups/about 1¼ lb/500 g
  raw vegetables, such as
  celery sticks, bell pepper
  strips, cucumber batons,
  sugar snap peas

Serves 8

Line a small, fine strainer with a piece of muslin, cheesecloth, or a new kitchen cloth. The shape of your strainer will determine the shape of the *labneh*—a conical shape is attractive. Set the strainer over a deep bowl so there is plenty of space for the whey to drain away and make sure there is room for it in your refrigerator.

Mix the yogurt thoroughly with chilis, citrus rinds, and a pinch of salt. Scoop the mixture into the strainer and smooth down. Cover with plastic wrap and place in the refrigerator for 24–36 hours. Turn out on to a plate and drizzle with olive oil. Arrange the vegetables around the *labneh* and serve.

per serving
**carbs: 3 g   protein: 3 g   calories: 58   fiber: 0 g   fat: 4 g (saturated fat: 2.5 g)**

# hot artichoke sin

**I call this "Sin" as a reminder that it is pure indulgence; that's also why it resides in the Party Food chapter. It is not particularly elegant-looking, but the taste never fails to please.**

**14 oz/400 g can artichoke hearts, drained and chopped**
**½ cup/4 fl oz/120 ml mayonnaise**
**⅔ cup/2 oz/50 g freshly grated Parmesan cheese**
**2 large green chilis, de-seeded and chopped**
**1 organic egg**

Serves 8

Preheat the oven to 425°F/220°C. Mix together the artichoke hearts, mayonnaise, cheese, and chilis in a bowl. Beat in the egg. Spread into a wide ovenproof dish in a layer no more than ¾ inch deep.

Bake the mixture for about 30 minutes, until bubbling and very dark golden on top and bottom. Remove from the oven and leave to cool.

To serve, slide on to a board and cut into bite-size squares with a knife or pizza-cutter.

**per serving**
**carbs: 5 g  protein: 5 g  calories: 176  fiber: 2 g  fat: 15 g (saturated fat: 3.5 g)**

# smoked eggplant purée

**This dip is also known as *Baba Ganoush*. Cooking the eggplant directly over a naked flame gives it a mystical smoky flavor, while softening it to a pulp. If you don't cook on gas, see instructions on how to oven-cook, below.**

2 medium eggplants
1 garlic clove
2 tbsp lemon juice
2 tbsp extra virgin olive oil
3 tbsp Greek (strained plain) yogurt
coarse salt and freshly ground black pepper

**to serve**
about 3 cups/1¼ lb/500 g raw vegetables, such as celery sticks, bell pepper strips, cucumber batons, Bibb lettuce leaves, Belgian endive leaves

Serves 8

Push a fork into the stem of an eggplant and hold directly in a high gas flame. Turn occasionally until completely soft and collapsed; the skin should be blackened to the point of ash in places, and steam should be escaping through the fork holes. Repeat with the second eggplant. Alternatively, preheat the oven to its highest setting. Prick the eggplants a few times, place on a cookie sheet and roast until completely soft.

Remove to a plate and leave to cool. Peel off the charred skins. Don't worry if a few little charred flecks remain as they will add to the flavor. Place the flesh in a bowl.

Crush the garlic clove with a little coarse salt in a mortar with a pestle for the best flavor. Alternatively, use a garlic crusher. Using a fork, break up the eggplants, then mash together with the crushed garlic and remaining ingredients, until fairly smooth. Season to taste.

**per serving**
**carbs: 2 g  protein: 1 g  calories: 41  fiber: 1.5 g  fat: 3.5 g (saturated fat: 0.7 g)**

# green bean and roasted bell pepper parcels

**Simplicity itself, beautiful to behold and even more gorgeous to eat. Don't save these just for a party—you should spoil yourself and your family with them, too, as a neat little appetizer or accompaniment. If you're really pressed for time, use broiled peppers from a jar, can, or deli—although fresh always tastes best.**

2 red bell peppers
⅔ cup/3½ oz/100 g fine green beans, trimmed
¼ cup/2 oz/50 g cream cheese
8 fresh basil leaves, shredded
sea salt and freshly ground black pepper

Makes 8

Preheat the broiler to its highest setting. Cut the bell peppers in half from stem to base and remove the cores and stems. Place, cut side down, on a cookie sheet lined with non-stick parchment. Broil the bell peppers until blackened and blistered all over. Remove to a plastic bag and seal. Leave to cool.

Meanwhile, bring a small pan of water to the boil and add salt. Cook the green beans for 2–3 minutes, until just tender but still bright green. Drain and cool under cold running water. Pat dry.

Peel the skins carefully off the bell peppers, taking care not to tear the flesh. Cut each half in half again from stem end to base. Lay on a board, peeled side down. Place about a rounded teaspoonful of cream cheese on the surface of each piece, then sprinkle basil over the cheese. Grind a little salt and pepper over them. Lay a bundle of 4–5 green beans across the top and wrap the bell pepper around the beans. Place seam side down on a plate and chill in the refrigerator until ready to serve.

**per serving**
**carbs: 3 g  protein: 1 g  calories: 48  fiber: 1 g  fat: 4 g (saturated fat: 2 g)**

Illustrated on *page 75*.

# 07: on the side

The best vegetarian food is a balanced composition of flavors and textures on the plate. None of these recipes need play second fiddle, but become part of a richly varied menu when paired up with other dishes.

# avocado and lemon salad

**Small pieces of whole lemon complement the creamy, rich avocado. Serve this with Red Bell Pepper and Goat's Cheese Timbales (see *page 35*).**

**1 lemon**
**2 ripe Hass avocados**
**pinch of salt**
**1 tsp finely grated fresh**
  **ginger**
**4 tbsp extra virgin olive oil**
**4 handfuls young spinach**
  **leaves, about 3½ oz/100 g**

Serves 4

Halve the lemon and squeeze the juice from one half into a small jug for the dressing. Cut the other in half again and then slice as thinly as possible.

Peel, halve and pit the avocados. Cut them into quarters, then slice.

Mix the salt and ginger into the lemon juice, then gradually whisk in the olive oil.

Arrange the spinach leaves on a platter or individual plates. Place the avocado and lemon slices on top. Drizzle the dressing over them and serve immediately.

**per serving**
**carbs: 2 g  protein: 2.5 g  calories: 247  fiber: 3 g  fat: 25 g (saturated fat: 4 g)**

# roasted eggplants with dill sauce

Here, the hot eggplants are doused in a cool, creamy sauce to create a warm salad—very nice in its own right, with crunchy lettuce leaves. Also try it with Halloumi-Stuffed Bell Peppers (see *page 36*) or Braised Fennel and Bell Peppers (see *page 106*).

2 large eggplants
olive oil, for brushing
1 cup/8 fl oz/250 ml Greek
   (strained plain) yogurt
3 tbsp chopped fresh dill, or
   2 tbsp freeze-dried dill
grated rind of 1 lemon
juice of ½ lemon
1 small garlic clove, crushed
salt and freshly ground
   black pepper

Serves 4

Preheat the oven to 425°F/220°C. Chop the stems off the eggplants and cut into six long wedges from top to bottom. Score the flesh diagonally without piercing the skin. Brush generously with olive oil and place, flesh side down, in a roasting pan. Season with salt and pepper. Roast for about 30 minutes, until soft and tinged with gold.

Meanwhile, make the sauce. Combine all the remaining ingredients thoroughly. Spoon the sauce over the hot eggplants and serve.

per serving
carbs: 4 g  protein: 4 g  calories: 115  fiber: 1 g  fat: 9 g (saturated fat: 5 g)

# braised fennel and bell peppers

**This bold and rustic Mediterranean side dish is the ideal foil for Arugula and Ricotta Cheesecake (see *page 55*), Roasted Eggplant with Dill Sauce (see *page 105*), or a plain omelet.**

3 tbsp olive oil
2 fennel bulbs, trimmed
  and sliced
1 red bell pepper, cored
  and sliced
1 yellow bell pepper, cored
  and sliced
3-4 fresh thyme sprigs
1 tsp coriander seeds
1 tsp chili flakes
10 large green pitted olives
2 garlic cloves, crushed
½ cup/4 fl oz/120 ml red
  wine
salt and freshly ground
  black pepper

Serves 4

Heat the oil in a wide skillet over a medium heat and add the fennel, bell peppers, and thyme. Cook, stirring frequently, until the vegetables are beginning to soften and brown.

Add the coriander seeds, chili flakes, and olives, season with salt and pepper and cook for a further 5 minutes. Add the garlic and cook very briefly until fragrant, then add the wine. Simmer until the liquid has evaporated.

per serving
**carbs: 6 g  protein: 1 g  calories: 136  fiber: 3 g  fat: 10 g (saturated fat: 1.5 g)**

# swiss chard with pine nuts and redcurrants

**Tart, blushing redcurrants are sublime with the earthy chard; a handful of cranberries could be substituted off-season—add them to the pan with the pine nuts. Serve this with Eggplant Rarebit (see *page 38*) or Creamy Celery Root Gratin (see *page 57*).**

3½ lb/1.5 kg swiss chard
   with stalks,
   or beet greens
½ cup/2 oz/50 g pine nuts
2 tbsp olive oil
1 cup/3½ oz/100 g
   redcurrants
salt and freshly ground
   black pepper

Serves 6

Wash and dry the chard or greens, strip leaves and chop coarsely. Chop the stalks into ¾ inch wide pieces.

Heat the oil in a pan and add the pine nuts. Cook, stirring, until the nuts are golden. Add the chard stalks, season with salt and pepper and stir. Cover the pan and cook, stirring occasionally, for about 3 minutes, until softened. Add chopped leaves, cover and cook until just wilted.

Transfer the mixture to a platter using a slotted spoon and sprinkle with the redcurrants.

**per serving**
**carbs: 8 g  protein: 6 g  calories: 153  fiber: 1 g  fat: 11 g (saturated fat: 1 g)**

# pumpkin and rutabaga mash

**This velvety purée is the ideal accompaniment to any particularly juicy dish. Try it with Portabello Mushrooms with Blue Cheese Custard (see *page 37*) or, if you're feeding a crowd, Provençal Tian (see *page 78*). The mash freezes well for future convenience.**

1¼ lb/500 g large pumpkin, trimmed weight, de-seeded, peeled and cubed
1¼ lb/500 g large rutabaga, trimmed weight, peeled and cubed
1 cup/8 fl oz/250 ml water
2 tbsp whipping cream
whole nutmeg, for grating
sea salt and freshly ground black pepper

Serves 6

Place the pumpkin and rutabaga in a pan and add water to cover and a pinch of salt. Cover, bring to the boil and cook for 20–30 minutes, until very tender and collapsing. Drain thoroughly (the cooking liquid is a delicious stock which you could save or freeze).

Return the vegetables to the pan and place over a low heat to steam off excess moisture for 5 minutes, stirring frequently. Remove the pan from the heat, add the cream and a very generous grinding of nutmeg. Mash to a smooth purée. Season to taste with salt and pepper and serve.

per serving
**carbs: 6 g  protein: 1 g  calories: 50  fiber: 2.5 g  fat: 2.5 g (saturated fat: 1 g)**

# turnip dauphinoise

I scanned dozens of French cookbooks searching for the ultimate Potato Dauphinoise recipe, but in the end I took a cue from stylish London cook Alastair Hendy, who makes a warm cream infusion and adds chives to his. Believe me, low-carb turnips plug into this classic dish like they were always meant to be there. To make life easy, use a food processor with a slicing blade for the turnips if you can.

1 tbsp/½ oz/15 g butter, for greasing

2¼ lb/1 kg turnips, trimmed weight, peeled and thinly sliced

1 large bunch of chives, chopped

1 garlic clove, halved

1 cup/8 fl oz/250 ml heavy or whipping cream

1 cup/8 fl oz/250 ml sour cream

½ cup/3½ fl oz/100 ml water

sea salt and freshly ground black pepper

Serves 6

Preheat the oven to 325°F/160°C. Butter a medium-sized gratin dish.

Make layers of turnip slices, sprinkling with salt, pepper, and chives as you go.

Place the garlic, cream, sour cream, and water in a small pan. Gradually bring to just before boiling point, stirring constantly, then remove from the heat. Pour the mixture over the turnips and discard the garlic.

Bake for 1¼–1½ hours, until the turnips are fork-tender throughout.

per serving
carbs: 10 g   protein: 3 g   calories: 349   fiber: 4 g   fat: 33 g (saturated fat: 20 g)

# greens in coconut milk

**Even those who need a little persuasion to eat their greens might find these hard to refuse. Use cabbage, or collard greens. Kale, Brussels sprout leaves and purple sprouting broccoli also like this treatment.**

1 tbsp olive oil
11 oz/300 g greens,
   trimmed weight, coarsely
   chopped or torn
1 inch piece of fresh
   ginger, chopped
14 fl oz/400 ml canned
   coconut milk
1 tsp ground cumin
sea salt and freshly ground
   black pepper

Serves 4

Heat a large pan over a medium heat and add the oil. Add greens and ginger, cover and cook, stirring occasionally, for about 2 minutes, until bright green and wilted.

Add the coconut milk and cumin, season with salt and pepper and cook, uncovered for 5 minutes. Serve hot.

per serving
**carbs: 5 g  protein: 5 g  calories: 222  fiber: 1.5 g  fat: 20 g (saturated fat: 12 g)**

# baby zucchini
# with mint and vinegar

When you see baby zucchini for sale, grab them. They are succulent and naturally sweet. If they have flowers attached, so much the better—this means that they are really fresh and you can add the flowers to this recipe, too. Bulk this up into a main course by adding some slices of buffalo mozzarella and a few arugula leaves.

2½ cups/1 lb 5 oz/600 g
   baby zucchini
2 tbsp olive oil
4 tsp white wine vinegar
a handful of fresh mint
   leaves, coarsely chopped
salt and freshly ground
   black pepper

Serves 4

If the zucchini really are young, there's no need to trim them, unless there is a withered flower on one end. If they are larger, trim both ends. Slice in half lengthways.

Heat the oil in a large, non-stick skillet over a low heat and gently cook the zucchini until well-colored on each side, then remove to a plate. You may have to do this in batches. As each batch comes out of the pan, sprinkle with a little vinegar and season with salt and pepper while still warm. Leave the zucchini to cool completely.

Sprinkle the chopped mint over them and finish with extra pepper.

**per serving**
**carbs: 2.5 g  protein: 2.6 g  calories: 76  fiber: 1.5 g  fat: 6 g (saturated fat: 1 g)**

# 08: sweet things

Got a sweet tooth? Satiate it here.

You needn't deny yourself an indulgent

dessert from time to time, with these

gratifying sugar-free treats.

# berry gratin

**To enjoy this at its absolute best, a powerful broiler is the key, so that the berries are quickly heated to the point of nearly bursting—then they collapse on the tongue.**

3½ cups/14 oz/400 g mixed
   berries, especially
   blackberries, raspberries,
   blueberries
4 tbsp sweetener
⅔ cup/5 oz/150 g cream
   cheese
5 tbsp whipping cream
juice of ½ lemon
coarsely grated rind of
   1 lemon

Serves 6

Preheat the broiler to its highest setting. Place the berries in a gratin dish and toss 1 tbsp of the sweetener through them.

Beat together the cream cheese, cream, the remaining sweetener and the lemon juice in a bowl. Spoon the mixture over the berries in an even layer covering most of the surface but leaving a border of berries around the edge. Sprinkle the lemon rind over the top.

Broil for about 5 minutes, or until the topping is patched with gold and the berries are swollen. Serve immediately.

**per serving**
**carbs: 4 g  protein: 2 g  calories: 174  fiber: 2 g  fat: 17 g (saturated fat: 10 g)**

# chocolate marzipan cheesecake

**A very indulgent cheesecake with a knock-out chocolate flavor and silky texture, perched on a marzipan base.**

**For the base**
½ cup/3½ oz/100 g
   ground almonds
¼ cup/2 oz/50 g butter,
   melted
2 tbsp sweetener
½ tsp almond extract
good pinch of salt

**For the topping**
1½ cups/12 oz/350 g cream
   cheese
⅔ cup/5 oz/150 g
   mascarpone cheese
6 tbsp sweetener
2 organic eggs
5 oz/150 g Belgian dark
   (bittersweet) diabetic
   chocolate, melted

Serves 10

Preheat the oven to 300°F/150°C. Put all the ingredients for the base in a bowl and stir to form a thick paste. Press firmly and evenly into the base of an 8-inch loose-based cake pan. Chill while you prepare the topping.

Beat together the two cheeses in a bowl with an electric whisk or process in a food processor. Beat in the sweetener and eggs and, finally, the chocolate, beating until smooth. Pour the mixture into the cake pan and bake for 30–40 minutes, until set but still slightly wobbly in the middle.

Leave to cool in the pan (it will set further as it cools). When completely cold, chill in the refrigerator for 3 hours or overnight.

**per serving**
**carbs: 6 g   protein: 7 g   calories: 402   fiber: 1 g   fat: 39 g (saturated fat: 21 g)**

# coconut ice cream

**This has to be the simplest ice cream ever. Remember to remove it from the freezer at least 30 minutes before serving, or longer. When stirred, you get a floppy, whipped texture just like soft ice cream from an ice cream vendor. Try it with a spoonful of Raspberry Purée (see *page 131*) drizzled over it. Yum! Yum!**

**14 fl oz/400 ml can coconut milk**
**1 cup/7 fl oz/200 ml heavy or whipping cream**
**6 tbsp sweetener**

Serves 8

Beat all the ingredients together until thoroughly combined. Chill in the refrigerator, then place in an ice cream maker and follow the manufacturer's instructions.

To freeze the ice cream manually, pour the chilled mixture into a large, shallow plastic container. Cover with a lid and place in the coldest part of the freezer for 1–1½ hours. Remove the container from the freezer and stir the mixture vigorously or beat with an electric mixer, incorporating the ice crystals that will have formed around the edge into the rest of the slush. Cover the container again and return it to the freezer. Repeat this twice more every 2 hours, or until the ice cream is thick throughout. Freeze until ready to serve, then leave at room temperature for at least 30 minutes. Stir before serving.

**per serving**
**carbs: 2.5 g  protein: 2 g  calories: 214  fiber: 0 g  fat: 22 g (saturated fat: 15 g)**

# coffee ice cream

**This is a traditional custard-based ice cream. Once you taste the custard, you may decide not to freeze it at all and simply devour it as a dessert—it's virtually irresistible.**

**1¼ cups/½ pint/300 ml whipping cream**
**3 organic egg yolks**
**3 tbsp sweetener**
**1 tbsp instant coffee powder**

Serves 4

Pour the cream into a pan and gradually bring to just below boiling point over a low to medium heat.

Meanwhile, whisk together the egg yolks, sweetener and instant coffee powder in a jug. The coffee may not immediately dissolve, but don't worry, it soon will.

When the cream just starts to bubble around the edges, remove from the heat and gradually pour it over the egg mixture, whisking constantly. Pour the mixture back into the pan and place it over a low heat. Continue whisking until the mixture becomes thick and coats the back of the spoon.

Pour the mixture back into the rinsed-out jug. Cover with plastic wrap and pierce the top so that the steam can escape. Cool, then chill in the refrigerator.

Pour into an ice cream maker and follow manufacturer's instructions. Alternatively, follow the instructions for manual ice cream making, as for Coconut Ice Cream (see *opposite*).

**per serving**
**carbs: 2 g  protein: 4 g  calories: 331  fiber: 0 g  fat: 34 g (saturated fat: 20 g)**

# lemon custard macaroon tart

**Dried coconut makes a perfect, golden, sweet and crispy tart base.**

2 cups/5½ oz/165 g
  dry shredded
  unsweetened coconut
2 organic eggs, separated
6 tbsp sweetener
butter, for greasing
½ cup/3½ fl oz/100 ml
  heavy or whipping cream
finely grated rind of
  2 lemons
juice of ½ lemon

Serves 8

Preheat oven to 350°F/180°C. Combine the coconut, egg whites and 3 tbsp of the sweetener in a bowl. Blend until well mixed and sticky. Generously grease an 8-inch loose-based, fluted quiche pan and press the coconut mixture firmly into the base and up the sides. Alternatively, use individual quiche pans or a non-stick muffin pan. Place on a cookie sheet and bake for 5 minutes.

To make the filling, beat together the egg yolks, the remaining sweetener, the cream, lemon rind, and juice. Remove the pie shell from the oven and pour in the filling. Return to the oven for 15 minutes, until patched with gold.

Leave to cool completely before removing from the pan. It might help to loosen the case by running the tip of a sharp knife all the way around the edge.

per serving
carbs: 1.5 g  protein: 3.5 g  calories: 205  fiber: 2.7 g  fat: 21 g (saturated fat: 15 g)

Illustrated on *page 76*.

# zabaglione

**There's a fair amount of continuous whisking involved in zabaglione, so it's most comfortably made for just two people. It should also be eaten immediately—warm, boozy and frothy. It's a wonderful spontaneous dessert.**

**4 organic egg yolks**
**2 tbsp sweetener**
**4 tbsp Marsala wine or**
   **Madeira or sherry**

Serves 2

Pour about a 1 inch depth of water into a pan over which you can set a small heatproof glass bowl. Bring to the boil.

Meanwhile, beat all ingredients together in the heatproof bowl until evenly combined. Reduce the boiling water to a simmer and set the bowl over it. Whisk constantly for 4–5 minutes, until the mixture has nearly trebled in volume and begins to hold its shape. Serve immediately on its own or with 1–2 spoonfuls of Raspberry Purée (see *page 131*) stirred through.

**per serving**
**carbs: 4 g  protein: 37 g  calories: 450  fiber: 0 g  fat: 27 g (saturated fat: 8 g)**

# cardamom cake

**Cardamom has the ability to make things taste sweeter, so I knew it would be ideal in a low-carb recipe. A sliver of this light sponge cake is perfect with coffee or afternoon tea.**

**butter, for greasing**
**⅔ cup/3 oz/75 g soy flour**
**½ cup/2 oz/50 g ground almonds**
**1 tsp baking powder**
**1 tsp cardamom seeds, out of the pod, crushed**
**5 tbsp sweetener**
**2 organic eggs**
**3 tbsp half-fat sour cream**
**3 tbsp sunflower oil**
**1 tbsp vanilla extract**
**generous pinch of salt**

Serves 8

Preheat the oven to 350°F/180°C. Grease an 8-inch cake pan and line the base with baking parchment.

Stir together the flour, ground almonds, baking powder, and cardamom seeds in a small bowl.

In a separate bowl, using an electric whisk or by hand, beat together the sweetener, eggs, sour cream, oil, vanilla, and salt. Stir the dry ingredients into the wet, combining thoroughly, but do not over-work. Pour into the prepared pan and bake for 20 minutes, until golden and set. Rest for 5 minutes, then turn out onto a wire rack to cool.

**per serving**
**carbs: 3 g  protein: 7.5 g  calories: 140  fiber: 5 g  fat: 11 g (saturated fat: 1.8 g)**

# cream cheese and macadamia nut brownies

**High-impact, real brownies—without the sugar.**

5 oz/150 g Belgian dark (bittersweet) diabetic chocolate, chopped
½ cup/3½ oz/100 g butter
3 organic eggs
5 tbsp sweetener
1 tsp vanilla extract
¾ cup/3 oz/75 g soy flour
1 tsp baking powder
pinch of salt
1 cup/3½ oz/100 g unsalted macadamia nuts, coarsely chopped
⅓ cup/3 oz/75 g chilled cream cheese, cut into small cubes

Makes 12

Preheat the oven to 350°F/180°C. Line a small rectangular cake pan or ovenproof dish with baking parchment.

Melt the chocolate and butter together in a heatproof bowl set over a pan of simmering water. Alternatively melt in the microwave. Stir until smooth, then leave to cool slightly.

Beat together the eggs, sweetener and vanilla in a large bowl. Add the chocolate mixture and combine thoroughly. Sift the flour, baking powder and salt over the mixture, add the nuts and stir until just mixed.

Pour into the prepared pan or dish and smooth the surface. Dot with the cream cheese. Bake for 30–40 minutes, until firm. Cool, then cut into 12 squares.

**per serving**
**carbs: 7 g  protein: 6 g  calories: 257  fiber: 1 g  fat: 23 g (saturated fat: 10 g)**

# rose and raspberry pudding

**The delicate taste of rosewater is the surprise element in this raspberry-flecked custard. I like to use frozen raspberries, because they ooze their magenta juices as they defrost in the cooling pudding.**

1 cup/5 oz/150 g fresh
   or frozen raspberries
6 organic egg yolks
4 tbsp sweetener
3 tbsp rosewater
2½ cups/1 pint/600 ml
   heavy or whipping cream
1 vanilla bean

Serves 6

Divide raspberries among 6 individual wine glasses or small bowls and set aside.

Place the egg yolks, sweetener and rosewater in a large bowl and hand-whisk until smooth.

Pour the cream into a pan. Slit the vanilla bean lengthways and scrape out the seeds into the cream, then place the bean in the cream and bring gently to just below simmering point—it should just start to bubble around the edges. Remove bean and gradually pour the hot cream over the egg mixture, whisking constantly. Pour the mixture back into the pan and whisk over a low heat until thick. Pour the custard into the prepared glasses or bowls. Leave to cool, then chill.

**per serving**
**carbs: 3 g  protein: 5 g  calories: 563  fiber: 0.6 g  fat: 60 g (saturated fat: 35 g)**

Illustrated on *page 76*.

# chocolate truffles

**These delectable truffles are the perfect little mouthful to round off dinner with a black coffee or brandy. If you use a high-quality diabetic chocolate, no-one will believe they're sugar-free. Wearing latex or plastic gloves makes rolling the truffle mixture easier. You will probably get through several changes of gloves.**

8 oz/250 g Belgian dark (bittersweet) diabetic chocolate, broken into pieces
¼ cup/2 oz/50 g butter
¾ cup/6 fl oz/175 ml heavy or whipping cream
6 tbsp unsweetened pure cocoa powder

Makes 35

Place the chocolate in a food processor and pulse until very finely chopped.

Place the butter and cream in a pan and heat gently just until the butter has melted. Remove the pan from the heat and stir in the chocolate. Continue to stir until smooth. If the mixture is too hot, it may separate; if this happens, add more cream.

Pour the mixture into a flat dish that will fit in the refrigerator. Leave to cool, then chill until firm.

Place the cocoa powder in a bowl. Remove the truffle mixture from the refrigerator. Scrape up cherry-size lumps of mixture and roll into smooth balls. Drop into the bowl of cocoa. Prepare a few at a time, shake them around in the cocoa to coat evenly, then remove to a plate. Continue until you have used up all of the truffle mixture.

Chill the truffles until ready to serve.

**per serving**
**carbs: 3 g  protein: 0.9 g  calories: 71  fiber: 0 g  fat: 6.3 g (saturated fat: 3.9 g)**

# pistachio meringues

**These are quite different from traditional meringues, but quite wonderful in their own right. They are feather-light and literally melt in the mouth while being crunchy at the same time. Pistachios make them extra special, but you could use hazelnuts or almonds instead.**

**1 cup/3½ oz/100 g pistachios, shelled**
**2 egg whites**
**pinch of cream of tartar**
**6 tbsp sweetener**

Makes 8

Preheat oven to 250°F/120°C. Line a cookie sheet with baking parchment.

Grind the pistachios to a powder in a food processor or chop as finely as possible by hand. Beat the egg whites with cream of tartar in a grease-free bowl until stiff. Beat in the sweetener. Gently fold in ground pistachios, keeping the mixture light and airy.

Spoon little mounds of the mixture on to the cookie sheet. Bake for 30 minutes, until crisp and golden.

**per serving**
**carbs: 1 g  protein: 3 g  calories: 78  fiber: 0.8 g  fat: 7 g (saturated fat: 1 g)**

# rhubarb fool

**Low-carb sweeteners taste particularly authentic with acidic foods, so rhubarb is a perfect foil and is itself low-carb. Ginger, also a great partner to rhubarb, makes this quintessentially English dessert complete.**

14 oz/400 g rhubarb,
  trimmed and cut into
  ½ inch pieces
3 tbsp water
2 tsp finely grated fresh
  ginger
pinch of salt
4 tbsp sweetener
1¼ cups/½ pint/300 ml
  heavy or whipping cream

Serves 6

Place the rhubarb, water, ginger and salt in a non-reactive pan (that is, not aluminium), cover and bring to the boil. Reduce the heat to a low simmer and stew for about 15 minutes, until the rhubarb has collapsed. Strain off some of the liquid through a non-aluminium sieve, then place in a ceramic or glass bowl and leave to cool.

When cool, add sweetener to taste. Whip the cream until it holds its shape, then fold in the rhubarb, so it streaks through the cream in pink ripples, but isn't completely homogenous. Spoon into four glasses and chill for at least 30 minutes before serving.

**per serving**
**carbs: 2 g  protein: 2 g  calories: 380  fiber: 1.5 g  fat: 40 g (saturated fat: 25 g)**

# raspberry mess

**Here's a rather nuttier version of the English summertime classic, made with Pistachio Meringues (see *opposite*). A touch of rosewater enhances the sweetness. Use strawberries instead of raspberries if that's what's available.**

1 recipe Pistachio
  Meringues (see *opposite*)
1 cup/8 fl oz/250 ml heavy
  or whipping cream
1 cup/5 oz/150 g raspberries
1 tsp rosewater

Serves 6

Whisk the cream until it holds its shape, but do not over-whisk.

Place the meringues in a large bowl and break up slightly. Add the raspberries and cream and fold through, trying not to flatten the meringues. Gently fold the rosewater through the mixture. Serve immediately.

**per serving**
**carbs: 3.3 g  protein: 6 g  calories: 484  fiber: 2.5 g  fat: 49 g (saturated fat: 26 g)**

# 09: flavor essentials

A few basics, with dressings and sauces specially designed to inject flavor, color and texture into just about anything that fails to excite. With these essential recipes in your repertoire you can create your own low-carb dishes.

# vegetable stock

Homemade vegetable stock will make your soups and stews taste better than a powder or cube, and will always be guaranteed virtually carb-less, if you follow my guidelines below. Alas, life doesn't always allow us the luxury of time to make it—but if you can make a large batch, freeze it in 1 cup/½ pint/250ml portions in zip-lock plastic bags. Also, save the water left from steaming and blanching vegetables and freeze the same way.

vegetables (see list below)
water (quantity to suit)
sea salt
peppercorns

**GOOD in stock:**
green onions
garlic
celery and celery leaves
parsley and parsley stems
leeks and well-washed
   leek greens
broccoli and broccoli stems
zucchini
fennel and fennel tops
turnips
woody herbs such as
   rosemary and thyme
bay leaves

**AVOID in stock:**
cabbage, spring greens,
   collard greens, kale
cauliflower
brussels sprouts
potatoes and any other
   starchy vegetables

Fill half a large pot with items from the "Good" list. Add enough water to cover the vegetables. Add sea salt to taste and a small handful of peppercorns. Bring to the boil and simmer for 20–30 minutes, then strain. Use immediately, or keep chilled for up to 3 days. Alternatively, freeze as described above.

per 1¼ cups/½ pint/300 ml serving
**carbs: 0.8 g  protein: 2 g  calories: 16  fiber: 0 g  fat: 0.2 g (saturated fat: 0 g)**

# paneer

This homemade curd cheese is a staple of the Indian diet. It's high in protein and has a wonderful creamy yet chewy texture. It is sold in some supermarkets and Asian groceries, but when you discover how easy it is to make yourself, you'll be a convert—all you have to do is separate milk into curds and whey. The homemade stuff is also infinitely lighter and creamier.

**15 cups/6 pints/3.5 liters whole milk**
**½ cup/3½ fl oz/100 ml strained freshly squeezed lemon juice**

Makes about 10½ oz/300 g

Bring the milk to the boil in a large pan. As soon as it starts to rise up the sides of the pan, turn off the heat. Stir in the lemon juice. Cover the pan and leave to stand for 10 minutes.

Drain the curds in a colander lined with cheesecloth or a clean dish cloth. When cool enough to handle, squeeze out the excess moisture and leave to cool and drain further, then chill.

Paneer can be used once it has cooled, although it will have a very crumbly texture. It will harden enough to slice within 1 hour in the refrigerator.

**per 3 oz/75 g serving**
**carbs: 2 g  protein: 9 g  calories: 76  fiber: 0 g  fat: 3 g (saturated fat: 1.5 g)**

# blender hollandaise

It's just about the most sinful sauce around—all that butter—but if you're sticking to your low-carb diet, a little of this won't blow it for you. This foolproof version has a particular affinity with steamed asparagus, and it's an essential part of Eggs Florentine (see *page 22*).

**3 organic egg yolks**
**2 tbsp water**
**1 tbsp fresh lemon juice**
**⅔ cup/5 oz/150 g lightly salted butter, diced**

Serves 4

Place the egg yolks, water and lemon juice in a blender.

Place the butter in a pan over a very low heat. As soon as it has melted, remove from the heat but do not let it cool.

Switch on the blender, then gradually pour the hot melted butter through the hole in the lid to produce a thick and creamy emulsion.

If the sauce needs to be kept for a short time before use, it can be poured into a heatproof bowl, covered and set over a pan of hot water (not actively simmering) to keep warm. It will solidify if stored in the refrigerator, but reheats successfully in a microwave.

per serving
**carbs: 0.2 g  protein: 2 g  calories: 325  fiber: 0 g  fat: 35 g (saturated fat: 20 g)**

# pesto

You may not be able to eat it with pasta (unless you've come across the low-carb pasta that's emerging on the market), but there's plenty else to enjoy pesto with. Try it stirred through spaghetti squash (see *page 58* for cooking instructions), boiled turnips, pumpkin or cauliflower, or as an uplifting companion for crunchy vegetables such as celery (see Celery with Pesto, *page 86*).

large bunch of fresh basil,
   stems and leaves, torn
1 cup/3½ oz/100 g
   pine nuts
2 garlic cloves
⅔ cup/2 oz/50 g freshly
   grated Parmesan cheese
6 tbsp olive oil
salt

Serves 4

Place the basil, pine nuts, garlic, Parmesan, and a pinch of salt in a food processor. Process until finely chopped, then, with the motor running, gradually add the oil. Taste for seasoning and add more salt if necessary. Store in and airtight container in the refrigerator for up to 3 days, or freeze.

per serving
carbs: 1 g  protein: 9 g  calories: 382  fiber: 0.5 g  fat: 38 g (saturated fat: 6 g)

# raspberry purée

This pink purée poses as a sweet sauce, flavoring (see Zabaglione, *page 119*) or low-carb jam substitute (see Cottage Cheese Pancakes, *page 26*).

½ cup/3 oz/75 g raspberries
1½ tbsp water
1 tbsp sweetener

Makes about
½ cup/4 fl oz/125 ml
Serves 4

Place all the ingredients in a blender and process until smooth. Pass through a sieve. The purée can be stored in the refrigerator for up to 3 days, or can be frozen.

per serving
carbs: 0.9 g  protein: 0.3 g  calories: 5  fiber: 0.5 g  fat: 0.1 g (saturated fat: 0 g)

# sweet chili sauce

This basic sauce is a perfect balance of sweet, sour, salty and hot—the principle behind the delicious flavor of South-east Asian food.

2 tbsp fresh lime juice
2 tbsp light soy sauce
2 tbsp sweetener
2 small red chilis,
   finely chopped
1 small garlic clove, crushed
   or finely grated

Combine all the ingredients. The heat will increase the longer it stands.

per serving
carbs: 0 g  protein: 0.2 g  calories: 3  fiber: 0.6 g  fat: 0 g (saturated fat: 0 g)

Serves 4

# coconut chili sauce

This is a fantastic marinade for tofu or a quick way to liven up steamed vegetables.
It's also delicious with hard-cooked eggs. It uses ready-made chili sauce so check the label to make sure it's a low-carb version with no sugar or modified starch.

5 tbsp coconut milk or
   coconut cream
2 tsp low-carb chili sauce
   or several shakes of
   Tabasco sauce
2 tsp light soy sauce
1 tsp fresh lime juice
1 tsp sweetener

Mix all ingredients together and serve. The sauce may solidify if it is kept in the refrigerator.

per serving
carbs: 1 g  protein: 0.6 g  calories: 35  fiber: 0 g  fat: 3.2 g (saturated fat: 2 g)

Serves 4

# basic vinaigrette

**A heavy mortar and pestle is one of the most useful tools in the kitchen. This is how you will get the very best flavor out of garlic as the base for any vinaigrette or sauce.**

1 garlic clove
1 tsp coarse sea salt
2 tbsp white wine vinegar
1 tsp dry mustard
½ tsp mixed dried herbs or
   Herbes de Provence
3 tbsp extra virgin olive oil
freshly ground black pepper

Serves 4

Using a mortar and pestle, pound the garlic with the salt until a smooth paste forms. Using the pestle, work in the vinegar, mustard, and herbs and season to taste with pepper. Gradually whisk in the olive oil.

per serving
**carbs: 0 g  protein: 0 g  calories: 75  fiber: 0 g  fat: 8 g (saturated fat: 1 g)**

# cheese sauce

**This rich sauce will make just about anything more exciting—try it spooned over a plate of steamed broccoli, zucchini, and hard-cooked eggs or smoked tofu.**

½ cup/4 fl oz/120 ml
   Vegetable Stock (see
   *page 128*)
½ cup/3½ oz/100 g
   cream cheese
½ cup/2 oz/50 g grated
   Gruyère cheese
½ tsp dry mustard (optional)
½ tsp fresh or dried thyme
   leaves (optional)

Serves 4

Bring the stock to the boil in a skillet. Add the cream cheese, breaking it up with a whisk. Whisk until smooth and melted.

Add the grated cheese, mustard, and thyme, if using, and whisk until the cheese has melted and the sauce is thick. Remove from the heat and serve immediately.

per serving
**carbs: 0.4 g  protein: 5 g  calories: 165  fiber: 0 g  fat: 16 g (saturated fat: 10 g)**

# italian blue cheese dressing

**The true, original blue cheese dressing—before it came out of labelled bottles—for all kinds of salads. Make sure the cheese is at room temperature before you start.**

3½ oz/100 g Gorgonzola
   cremosa or
   Dolcelatte cheese
1 tbsp white wine vinegar
2 tbsp extra virgin olive oil
sea salt and freshly ground
   black pepper

Serves 4

Remove and discard any rind from the cheese. Place the cheese in a bowl and break it up slightly with a fork, then beat in the vinegar. Beat in the oil with a pinch of salt and pepper. This dressing will keep in the refrigerator for up to 3 days.

**per serving**
**carbs: 0.2 g  protein: 6 g  calories: 152  fiber: 0 g  fat: 14 g (saturated fat: 6.5 g)**

# sesame vinaigrette

**A light salad dressing with an Asian twist, this is also another good tofu marinade.**

1 tbsp sesame seeds
2 tbsp dark soy sauce
2 tbsp rice vinegar
2 tbsp sesame oil

Makes about
½ cup /3½ fl oz/100 ml
Serves 4

Place the sesame seeds in a small, dry skillet and set over a medium heat. Cook, shaking the pan frequently, until the seeds are popping and golden. Transfer to a bowl and leave to cool.

Beat the remaining ingredients into the toasted sesame seeds. Use immediately, while the seeds are still crunchy.

**per serving**
**carbs: 0.6 g  protein: 1 g  calories: 75  fiber: 0.3 g  fat: 8 g (saturated fat: 1 g)**

# sesame mayo

Here's an example of how the magical combination of three ingredients adds up to more than the sum of its parts. This versatile sauce/dressing/dip just goes with everything!

3 tbsp sesame seeds
½ cup/4 fl oz/120 ml
  mayonnaise
1½ tbsp dark soy sauce

Makes ½ cup/4 fl oz/120 ml
Serves 4

Place the sesame seeds in a small, dry skillet and set over a medium heat. Cook, shaking the pan frequently, until the seeds are popping and golden. Transfer to a bowl and leave to cool.

Add the mayonnaise and soy sauce and combine thoroughly. The sauce is best eaten on the day you make it, as the sesame seeds tend to become soggy after a while.

per serving
carbs: 0.3 g  protein: 1 g  calories: 137  fiber: 0.3 g  fat: 15 g (saturated fat: 2 g)

# satay sauce

This sauce or dressing provides a speedy flavor injection. Make a quick "gado-gado" salad with hard-cooked eggs, lettuce or shredded cabbage, bean sprouts, a few bell pepper strips, and sliced green onions, then smother it in this dressing.

3 tbsp crunchy unsweetened
  peanut butter
2 tbsp boiling water
2 tsp low-carb store-bought
  chili sauce
1 tsp fresh lime juice
1 tsp sweetener

Makes about
½ cup/3½ fl oz/100 ml
Serves 4

Place the peanut butter in a small bowl and pour over the boiling water. Beat with a fork until thoroughly combined. Beat in the remaining ingredients and taste for seasoning.

per serving
carbs: 1 g  protein: 2 g  calories: 50  fiber: 0.5 g  fat: 4 g (saturated fat: 1 g)

# menu ideas

**brunch buffet**
japanese omelet
(*page 20*)
blueberry almond griddle
cakes (*page 18*)
almond muffins with butter
(*page 27*)
melon berry power
smoothie (*page 19*)
black coffee

**picnic**
tunisian spiced torte
(*page 62*)
marinated crudité salad
(*page 91*)
cream cheese and
macadamia nut
brownies (*page 121*)
iced tea with lemon
and sweetener

**mediterranean meze**
olive raisins (*page 88*)
halloumi-stuffed bell
peppers (*page 36*)
smoked eggplant purée
(*page 100*)
citrus chili labneh platter
(*page 98*)
fruity red wine

**lunch buffet**
portabello mushrooms
with blue cheese
custard (*page 37*)
provençal tian (*page 78*)
avocado and lemon salad
(*page 104*)
chocolate marzipan
cheesecake (*page 115*)

**al fresco lunch**
spanish tortilla with
zucchini and manchego
(*page 51*)
green bean and roasted
bell pepper parcels
(*page 101*)
a crisp green salad served
with italian blue cheese
dressing (*page 134*)
chilled prosecco

**easy asian buffet**
tofu, mint and palm
heart salad (*page 45*)
vietnamese asparagus
pancakes (*page 54*)
*gado-gado* salad (see
satay sauce intro,
*page 135*)
coconut ice cream
(*page 116*)

**lunch box**
spanish tortilla with
zucchini and manchego
(*page 51*)
spicy tofu jerky
(*page 90*)
almond muffin (*page 27*)

**warming winter lunch**
curried celery root soup
with cilantro oil
(*page 43*)
warm salad of eggplant
and melting camembert
(*page 56*)
zabaglione (*page 119*)

**speedy after-work dinner 1**
chinese-spice tofu
and mesclun salad
(*page 46*)
egg foo yung (*page 64*)

**speedy after-work dinner 2**
egg flower soup (*page 31*)
warm exotic mushroom
salad (*page 47*)

**thai feast**
cucumber and tofu
satay (*page 94*)
fragrant coconut broth
(*page 32*)
thai hot and sour salad
with crispy tofu
(*page 59*)
coconut ice cream
(*page 116*)
jasmine tea

**indian feast**
spiced charred eggplants
(*page 39*)
paneer and herb fritters
(*page 80*)
pumpkin curry (*page 81*)
rose and raspberry
pudding (*page 122*)
low-carb beer

**cocktail bash**
chili-crust brazil nuts
(*page 86*)
saffron aïoli with quail's
eggs and asparagus
(*page 96*)
eggplant and smoked
cheese involtini
(*page 95*)
cucumber with pink
pickled ginger
(*page 97*)
chocolate truffles
(*page 123*)
vodka martinis

**4-course red carpet dinner**
tricolore skewers (with
champagne) (*page 97*)
red bell pepper and goat's
cheese timbales
(*page 35*)
warm poached egg salad
with tarragon vinaigrette
(*page 48*)
chilled white burgundy
individual berry gratins
(*page 114*)
cognac and black coffee

# index

Published in the U.S. and Canada by Whitecap Books Ltd. For more information, contact Whitecap Books, 351 Lynn Avenue, North Vancouver, British Columbia, Canada, V7J 2C4 www.whitecap.ca

First published in Great Britain in 2004 by PAVILION BOOKS

An imprint of **Chrysalis** Books Group

The Chrysalis Building
Bramley Road, London W10 6SP

© Pavilion Books, 2004
Text © Celia Brooks Brown, 2004
Photography © Pavilion Books, 2004

EDITOR AND PROP STYLIST:
Emily Preece-Morrison
DESIGNER: Lotte Oldfield
PHOTOGRAPHER: Tara Fisher
FOOD STYLIST:
Celia Brooks Brown
NUTRITIONIST: Fiona Hunter

ISBN 1-55285-617-8

Library of Congress Cataloging-in-Publication Data available upon request.
10 9 8 7 6 5 4 3 2 1

Printer: Times Offset, Malaysia

# for christiane

## author's acknowledgments

Massive thanks to Katharina, Jan and all the Childwickbury guinea pigs. I couldn't have done this without you. Tracy, you've now got that low-carb shopping list down pat! Thanks for making life so easy in my favorite kitchen. Thanks Paula, for always sorting out the nuts and bolts for lunch while I'm scrambling to the finish line.

Fiona Hunter, you were quite simply a godsend. Without your skills and advice, writing this book would have been a chore. Thank you hundreds of times over.

Kate Oldfield, thanks for believing in me, and running with this idea in such a hurry.

Emily Preece-Morrison, you are an absolute delight to work with. Thanks for your patience—you have been my rock. Lotte, it's been a privilege to have your talented eye on board.

Tara Fisher, thank you. You brought beauty to this book.

Jennifer Joyce, thanks for all the comforting chats and for letting me pinch your recipe.

Norman Fu, thanks for the Foo Yung advice—it was a revelation. Ian Fenn, thank you for putting me in touch with Norman.

Jane Hall, thanks for your kind words and for relaying your experiences.

Sophie Duvall, thank you angelight!

Tou at Number One Café, 1 Dalgarno Gardens, London W10—I may have moved across town but your exquisite Thai food still inspires me.

Thai Café, Northwold Road, Stoke Newington, London N16, thanks for the rutabaga.

Jeanne, Rupert, Jessica, Sorrel and Romilly, thanks for putting up with Cyclone Celia in the Dean Farm kitchen.

Mom, Dad, Amy, Bethie, thanks for your love and support. Ame, I really appreciate your input.

Dan and Paulie, you are both quite certainly neither vegetarian nor low-carbers, but thanks for the constructive critiques. Many more such meals to come, out of the freezer. Big love.

## publisher's acknowledgments

Many thanks to everyone who has assisted with the making of this book: Mark Latter, Sue Rowlands, China & Co., the staff at Ceramica Blue, 10 Blenheim Crescent, London W11, for the loan of beautiful china and linen for the photoshoot, Linda Doeser and Caroline Hamilton.